FOREWORD
COUNCILLOR FR HAEBERLING, LEADER, BATH AND NORTH EAST SOMERSET COUNCIL

**Creating the Canvas for Public Life in Bath –
Public Realm and Movement Strategy
for Bath City Centre**

This is an ambitious document which reflects the Council's commitment to improving the distinctiveness, vitality and sustainability of our city and district.

It puts forward a bold, long-term plan for a world-class city centre, which can be delivered over the next 10 to 20 years as funding and investment are secured.

It is designed to give pedestrians, cyclists and public transport vehicles priority over cars, and deliver a network of beautiful, refashioned streets and public spaces. The aim is to encourage more vibrant and diverse public life within the streets, spaces, parks and gardens of the city centre and along its River Corridor, creating new opportunities for social interaction, creativity and play and helping make the city a more active, inclusive and engaging place.

This, we believe, will benefit local people, stimulate further economic investment and business growth, and enhance Bath's status as a UNESCO World Heritage Site and international visitor destination.

These proposals are firmly rooted in an understanding and appreciation of Bath's history and evolution as a city and seek to deliver distinctive, modern solutions that respect the city's unique character.

We do not underestimate the challenge of delivering the strategy; it will demand significant on-going public and private sector investment, further improvements in transport infrastructure and strong leadership.

The Council is looking to release capital resources to invest in the public realm. Other landowners, investors, developers and public sector funding bodies will also be required to play their part in delivering the long-term plan.

Nevertheless, the Council is keen to implement this strategy and a programme of projects is already underway. Similar studies are under development for Keynsham, Midsomer Norton and Radstock, and in time some of the proposals for the city and town centres, particularly in relation to pedestrian and cycle movement, will hopefully expand into surrounding neighbourhoods.

We believe this plan will help us achieve our vision of making Bath and North East Somerset an even better place to live, work and visit.

Francine Haeberling

Councillor Francine Haeberling
Leader, Bath and North East
Somerset Council

INTRODUCTION

The public realm offers spaces for enjoyment, entertainment and social interaction and quieter areas for those who value solitude. Public space is open and free to use. It provides an essential opportunity for all parts of society, to meet, mingle and connect.

Throughout the history of civilisation, the public realm – the shared space between buildings – has been a focal point for public life. The squares, promenades, streets, lanes, markets, parks and riversides of our city and town centres are where people have always gathered to meet others, to demonstrate and campaign, to barter and trade, to parade and play, to share their grief and to celebrate.

The public realm offers spaces for enjoyment, entertainment and social interaction and quieter areas for those who value solitude and contemplation. Public space is open and free to use. It provides an essential opportunity for all parts of society, for the familiar and the foreign, to mingle and connect.

Over the past century, the increasing dominance of the motor car has done much to damage the character and quality of public space and public life across the world.

However, in recent decades a growing number of pioneering cities such as Copenhagen, Freiburg and Bordeaux have succeeded in reversing the hierarchy of car and pedestrian within their centres and are rediscovering the benefits of putting people and sense of place at the heart of urban life. The increase in economic success, popularity and wellbeing that these and other cities have subsequently experienced provides inspiration and guidance when considering and planning the future of Bath's city centre.

The strategy
Creating the Canvas for Public Life in Bath – Public Realm and Movement Strategy for Bath City Centre recommends a radical and inspirational plan for the transformation of Bath's urban environment. Although ambitious and aspirational, it is also pragmatic and flexible and can be delivered on an incremental basis over the next 10 to 20 years.

The strategy puts forward a series of measures to address traffic movement within and around the centre of the city in order to establish a network of beautiful new and reclaimed public spaces, successful streets and an enhanced River Corridor. It also recommends a programme of improvements to simplify, refashion and manage the public realm, including the removal of street clutter and the introduction of a new bespoke range of street furniture and pedestrian wayfinding products to enhance, reveal and communicate the distinctiveness and diversity of Bath.

The ultimate objective of the Public Realm and Movement Strategy is to stimulate a rediscovery of a vibrant public life within the city centre and to enhance the enormous potential of Bath as a place, not just for the benefit of visitors and businesses, but for the enjoyment, health and wellbeing of the community as a whole.

CREATING THE CANVAS FOR PUBLIC LIFE IN BATH

Policy context

The strategy responds to the Council's vision for Bath and North East Somerset as 'a distinctive place, with vibrant and sustainable communities where everyone fulfils their potential' and to a number of corporate improvement priorities including 'Sustainable Growth', 'Improving Transport and the Public Realm', 'Building communities where people feel safe and secure' and 'Addressing the causes and effects of climate change'.

It builds upon the Local Strategic Partnership's Sustainable Community Strategy, the Bath and North East Somerset Local Plan and the Council's Future for Bath vision and has been developed alongside a series of related strategies and studies for retail, culture, destination management and business growth. Subject to further testing and integration, these studies will contribute to a new planning policy framework (Bath and North East Somerset Core Strategy and Local Development Framework) and a Regeneration Delivery Plan for Bath.

The strategy has been subject to a Sustainability Appraisal to ensure that sustainable development considerations are properly integrated. Where appropriate the recommended changes have been included within relevant sections of the strategy, however many of the changes relate to the implementation of specific projects rather than the strategy itself. In these circumstances the Council will refer to the Sustainability Appraisal during the preparation and implementation of these projects.

Status

This strategy has been approved as Council policy. It will be a material consideration in the planning process and will directly inform the Council's review of the Bath and North East Somerset Supplementary Planning Document for Planning Obligations.

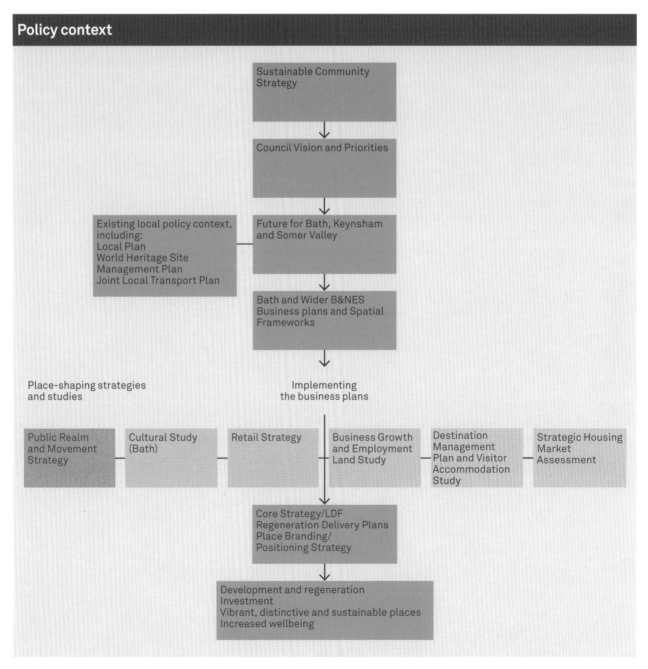

Policy context

- Sustainable Community Strategy
- Council Vision and Priorities
- Existing local policy context, including:
  Local Plan
  World Heritage Site Management Plan
  Joint Local Transport Plan
- Future for Bath, Keynsham and Somer Valley
- Bath and Wider B&NES Business plans and Spatial Frameworks

Place-shaping strategies and studies

Implementing the business plans

- Public Realm and Movement Strategy
- Cultural Study (Bath)
- Retail Strategy
- Business Growth and Employment Land Study
- Destination Management Plan and Visitor Accommodation Study
- Strategic Housing Market Assessment

- Core Strategy/LDF Regeneration Delivery Plans Place Branding/ Positioning Strategy

- Development and regeneration Investment
  Vibrant, distinctive and sustainable places
  Increased wellbeing

The proposals within this document take full account of, and seek to deliver a range of public realm objectives within the City of Bath World Heritage Site Management Plan, particularly the sections on Physical Access, Interpretation and Visitor Management. They also fully engage with the implications of the £54 million Bath Transport Package bid to the Department for Transport and the EC CIVITAS initiative.

Who is it for?
The ideas and proposals within the Public Realm and Movement Strategy are relevant to anyone with an interest in the future of the city centre. The strategy has been developed with the involvement of a number of key community stakeholders and Council members and officers.

What happens next?
The Public Realm and Movement Strategy will be implemented through the Council's Public Realm and Movement Programme. A detailed delivery plan and funding strategy are currently being prepared for the next five years.

This will include the development of a Bath Pattern Book to establish a much needed design tool to inform, guide and regulate the development of Bath's public realm in the future. This will include details of paving, street furniture, wayfinding, lighting, public art, soft landscaping and tree planting.

Extended
study area

City centre
study area

2km

4km

DOCUMENT SUMMARY

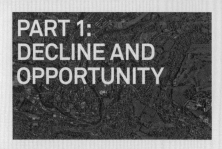

PART 3: A CITY REBALANCED, REFASHIONED, REVEALED AND REANIMATED

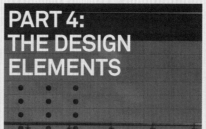

PART 4: THE DESIGN ELEMENTS

PART 5: REALISING THE STRATEGY

PART 1:
DECLINE AND
OPPORTUNITY

THE DECLINE OF THE PUBLIC REALM

THE OPPORTUNITY
THE CASE FOR TRANSFORMING BATH
BEING INFORMED BY THE PAST
REINFORCING BATH'S DNA
THE ESSENCE OF BATH

THE DECLINE OF THE PUBLIC REALM

Like an orchestra without a conductor, the city's public realm currently lacks unity of design and direction.

The decline of the public realm

The natural beauty of Bath's landscape setting, the elegance of its Georgian architecture and the theatricality of its built form endure and continue to delight. However, few could claim today that the streets and spaces which unify its buildings and form the platform for public life and movement within the centre are worthy of Bath's status as a World Heritage Site and international visitor destination.

The decline of the public realm has occurred slowly, almost imperceptibly over decades. Incrementally, many of the special qualities for which Bath's city centre was once envied and emulated, such as its sense of order, coherence, clarity of design and quality have eroded, gradually undermining the distinctiveness, reputation and economic potential of Bath as a place. Like an orchestra without a conductor, the city's public realm currently lacks unity of design and direction and its former sense of a total composition has become diminished.

Constricted movement

In response to the difficulty of accommodating ever-increasing levels of vehicular traffic within the centre, the inherent qualities of a number of Bath's historic streets and spaces have gradually eroded, at times creaking with the competing demands of cars, buses, coaches and heavy goods vehicles. As well as constricting the flow of pedestrian movement, this can generate high levels of air pollution and at times unnecessary tension and stress for drivers and pedestrians. In places, crowded footways or mean pavement widths regularly force people into the highway with potentially perilous consequences. Over recent years efforts to calm traffic in some areas of the centre have in part been successful, but many of those streets and spaces still remain characterised by tarmacadam and highway paraphernalia, which, while sometimes a legal requirement, do little to engender a positive sense of place.

The city centre also lacks clear, welcoming gateways and arrival points for pedestrians, and those few that exist display a visually inconsistent variety of maps and signs, compounding a sense of disorder. The absence of a clear and coherent pedestrian information and navigation system (often referred to as 'wayfinding') limits the opportunity for people to circulate around and beyond the centre on foot. When combined with the shortage of high quality public spaces, this often results in overcrowding and congestion in the few successfully pedestrianised areas around the Abbey, Roman Baths and parts of Stall Street.

Similarly, insufficient recognition and access is given to cyclists within the centre, limiting the potential of another healthy and non-polluting form of movement. While Bath is fortunate to benefit from higher levels of public transport use than many other cities, it is a challenge for the uninitiated to easily understand and access the city's bus network.

Lost spaces

It is surprising that in an international visitor destination and spa resort which many regard as the birthplace of 18th century urbanism and promenading, there are today so few successful and enjoyable urban spaces within the centre for people to gather with friends, to eat and drink, to be entertained, to play, and to watch the world go by. Much of this can be blamed on the rise of vehicular movement which led to some of Bath's finest set pieces such as Terrace Walk, Orange Grove, High Street and Queen Square becoming spaces for cars and not people.

Perhaps Bath's greatest lost (or never properly discovered) space and certainly its most neglected asset is the River Avon, whose winding course still defines the form and boundary of much of the city centre. No longer a vital transport route, it is to be lamented that today's river remains in large parts unattractive, inaccessible and under-utilised.

Clutter and disorder

Along with many other towns and cities, Bath has, over recent decades, failed to grasp the value and importance of its public realm as an arena for public life and wellbeing and as a generator of economic vitality and success. Years of under-investment and insufficient management have seen the once celebrated public spaces, parades and passages of the 18th century city become increasingly tired, cluttered and incoherent.

A closer inspection at street level reveals a cacophony of dated street furniture and poorly maintained surfaces including cracked and patched paving, pseudo-Victorian benches and finger posts, rusting litter bins, and a proliferation of poles and highways signage. Recent attempts to improve areas of public realm at Milsom Street and Kingsmead Square were carried out in the absence of a complete strategy and, despite their respective merits, have therefore contributed little towards the clarity and coherence of the city centre as a whole.

The factors outlined above reflect the current imbalance between the needs for vehicular access and the quality and experience of the pedestrian environment. They also highlight the slow erosion of the qualities of place which once made Bath unique, weakening its distinctiveness and attractiveness at a time when it faces increasing competition from other cities.

THE DECLINE OF THE PUBLIC REALM

Few could claim that the treatment of the city's streets and spaces are worthy of Bath's World Heritage Site status.

Bath's sense of order, coherence and design have gradually eroded.

The dominance of traffic can constrict pedestrian movement.

Many streets and spaces are characterised by tarmac and highway paraphernalia.

The city centre lacks clear, welcoming gateways and arrival points for pedestrians.

There are too few successful urban public spaces for people to enjoy within the centre.

The public realm has suffered from decades of under-investment and insufficient management.

There is a cacophony of dated street furniture and poorly maintained surfaces including cracked and badly patched paving.

Air pollution is a growing problem.

THE OPPORTUNITY
THE CASE FOR
TRANSFORMING BATH

Bath currently stands on the threshold of a major cycle of change and investment in the city centre. This provides a once in a lifetime opportunity to look at the centre of Bath as a whole and to develop a coherent long-term vision and delivery plan for its revitalisation.

The case for transforming Bath

Looked at in isolation, the scale and extent of the decline and disorder within Bath's public realm represents a sobering, if not overwhelming, challenge for the public and private sectors to overcome. Even taking account of the impacts of the current economic downturn, in the longer-term Bath stands on the threshold of a major cycle of change and investment in the city centre as it responds to the Government's growth agenda, as a result of the Regional Spatial Strategy and its own identified need for economic, physical and cultural regeneration and renewal. This provides a once in a lifetime opportunity to look at the centre of Bath as a whole and to develop a coherent long-term vision and delivery plan for its revitalisation.

Future for Bath

The case for change was originally highlighted in the Council's Future for Bath vision of 2007 (www.bathnes.gov.uk/future/bath). This established a range of significant socio-economic and physical challenges facing the city and in particular the city centre, and outlined the opportunity to actively harness and shape the housing and economic growth agenda in order to secure a more successful, sustainable and distinctive future. The Future for Bath has directly informed the recent

Bath and North East Somerset Sustainable Community Strategy and Core Strategy.

According to the Future for Bath Business Plan by Ernst and Young and the recent Economic Strategy for Bath and North East Somerset, Bath's future economic prosperity and sustainability depends on attracting higher value employers and jobs in order to rebalance the current low-wage economy. The Vision and Economic Strategy promote the development of a distinctive local economy where higher value knowledge, creative and environmental industries, including owner-managed companies, are actively targeted and encouraged. They also promote the delivery of new, contemporary homes, including affordable housing, to accommodate existing demand within the city and to house an expanded workforce.

At the same time the city is seeking to create a higher quality visitor economy where people stay for longer and where health and wellbeing (associated with the Spa) and the lucrative conference and business tourism markets are developed.

A high quality, contemporary public realm must be part of the strategy to attract new knowledge-based and creative industries to the city and to widen Bath's appeal to more high-spend, younger cultural visitors.

below
Plan showing major
areas of agreed and
potential change

key

1. The Podium
2. Guildhall/Riverside/Rugby Club
3. Manvers Street
4. SouthGate/Bath Spa Station
5. Bath Quays
6. Kingsmead/James Street
7. Charlotte Street Car Park
8. Bath Western Riverside
9. Twerton Riverside

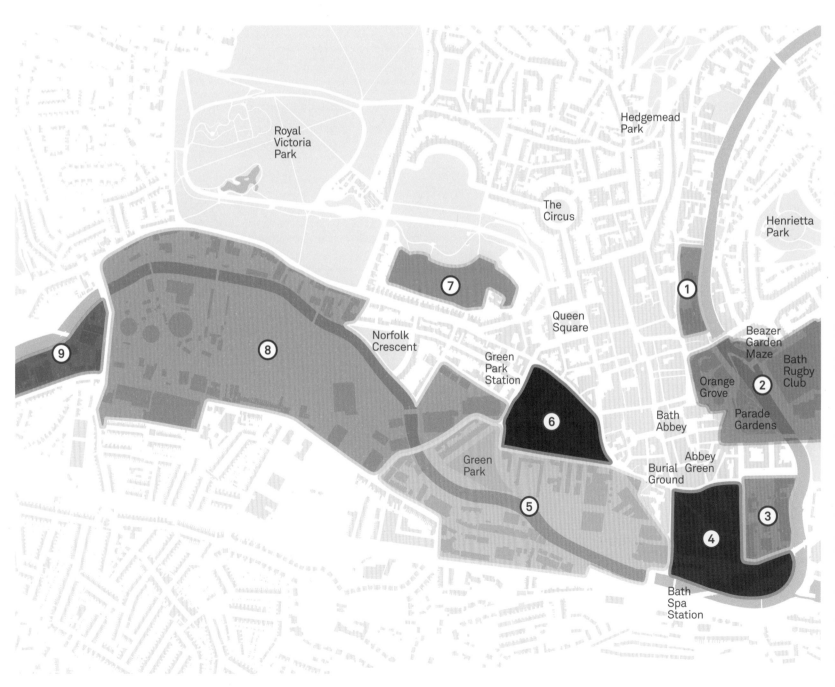

This could offer the buzz and excitement of contemporary artistic and cultural expression, alongside the city's existing outstanding offering of heritage and traditional culture.

Bath needs to attract younger, more innovative and creative people in order to sustain its future economy – people who may currently perceive the city as a place for middle-aged and elderly people. This strategy delivers a more balanced and successful city centre. It envisages a Bath where traditional and contemporary values of design and culture are fused and where people of all ages and backgrounds can enjoy a rich and varied experience.

Central to this work is the principle that the regeneration of the city centre must be inspired and guided by Bath's unique qualities and values, its DNA, as a place. It must also embrace current ethical and environmental concerns, including the need to build a low carbon economy in response to climate change, and changing patterns of consumption, work and behaviour within society.

The Future for Bath paints a picture of the type of city Bath has the potential to become: ...a vibrant, confident and highly distinctive city with a successful and sustainable economy, strong ethical values, high quality and popular public spaces, an attractive River Corridor and a happier and more fulfilled community. It enjoys a strong regional, national and international identity, built upon Bath's beauty, heritage and essential character. It is easy to access and move around by public transport, on foot or by bicycle. It balances the needs of local residents, workers and visitors and is recognised around the world as a leading centre for water and wellbeing, pleasure and culture, imagination and design, and knowledge and invention.

Public Realm and Movement Strategy

The Public Realm and Movement Strategy is one of the most significant components in the delivery of this long-term vision. With major development schemes coming forward in future years adding new urban quarters and new forms of architecture to the mix of the existing city centre, it is more urgent than ever for Bath to look 20 years or more ahead to the completion of its expanded centre and to plan now for the type of place it wants to become.

This strategy provides the opportunity to consider the future of the city centre in a holistic way. It advocates a long-term plan and investment strategy for public realm and movement, which builds incrementally towards the completion of an integrated and coherent centre where the needs of vehicular access and the needs of the pedestrian and cyclist are rebalanced; and where a simple, beautiful, high quality public realm blends old and new together into a unified whole.

This approach is underpinned by the belief that the qualities of a place, particularly its public realm, can have a profound impact on individuals and communities and is a key factor in personal and collective wellbeing and economic success. In Bath's case, it proposes that wellbeing should be placed at the centre of a sequential process that will:

Level 1 Transform the public realm to revitalise the city centre to a standard that reflects its status as an international visitor destination and World Heritage Site.

Level 2 Transform the economic, social and cultural wellbeing of Bath's communities, businesses and institutions.

Level 3 Lead to long-term competitive advantage through positioning Bath as a city that offers an exemplary 21st century sustainable lifestyle.

Seen in this context, there is a compelling case for transforming Bath's public realm. It provides the opportunity to re-unify the quality of buildings and their immediate and wider settings, to dramatically improve the experience of the city centre for the pedestrian, to enhance the attractiveness and competitiveness of Bath as a city; to integrate the old and new parts of the centre, to be a catalyst for further economic investment and vitality; to encourage healthier lifestyles; to increase community safety and ultimately to build an experience of public-life and wellbeing which could become one of the city's defining features.

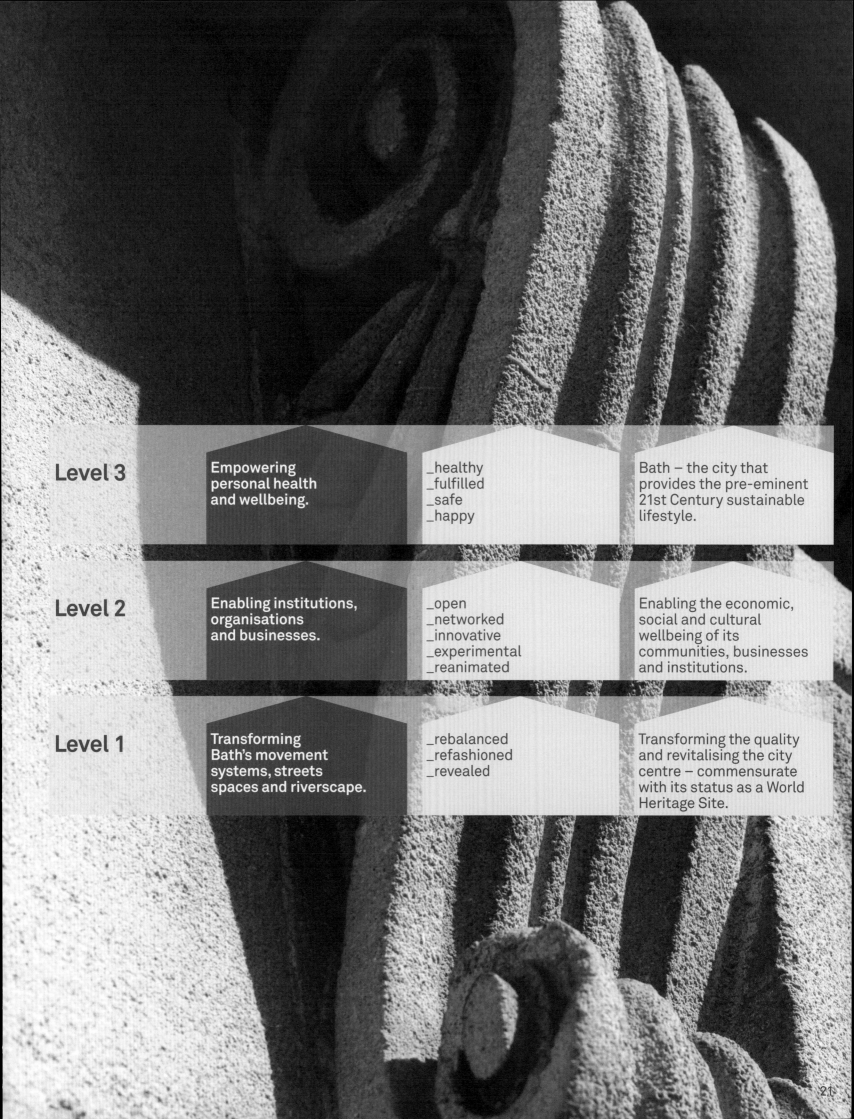

Level 3	Empowering personal health and wellbeing.	_healthy _fulfilled _safe _happy	Bath – the city that provides the pre-eminent 21st Century sustainable lifestyle.
Level 2	Enabling institutions, organisations and businesses.	_open _networked _innovative _experimental _reanimated	Enabling the economic, social and cultural wellbeing of its communities, businesses and institutions.
Level 1	Transforming Bath's movement systems, streets spaces and riverscape.	_rebalanced _refashioned _revealed	Transforming the quality and revitalising the city centre – commensurate with its status as a World Heritage Site.

THE OPPORTUNITY
BEING INFORMED BY THE PAST

With its inspirational urbanism and architecture, its spa waters and status as a centre for culture, pleasure and fashion, Bath once kept ahead of all possible competitors and its economy thrived. Its successes were admired and copied by many larger cities, including London.

Bath is one of the world's most beautiful cities

In 1987 the entire city was inscribed on the United Nations' Educational, Scientific and Cultural Organisation's (UNESCO) list of World Heritage Sites in recognition of its 'outstanding universal values'.

This designation pays tribute to Bath's fascinating social history and to a range of remarkable features including its three hot springs, its Roman archaeology and, not least, the harmony of sublime landscape setting, urban design, architecture and materials which so successfully reinvented the city in the 18th century.

Indeed, by the end of that century, Bath was a recognised leader in the art of city-making, having transformed itself from a rather muddled, cluttered and economically uncertain medieval town into an elegant, imposing and ordered contemporary city: 'Towards 1800 Bath was being touted as 'the most admired City in Europe' a beautiful urban artefact in its own right' [1]

With its inspirational urbanism and architecture, its spa waters and its status as a centre for culture, pleasure and fashion, Bath kept ahead of all possible competitors and its economy thrived. It was frequented by royalty, the aristocracy and glitterati of the day and its successes were admired and copied by many larger cities, including London. Today, as Bath comes to terms with the need to physically and economically revitalise and refashion its public realm and movement systems, there are many interesting and relevant lessons to be learned from its 18th century renaissance.

Contemporary city

Although classically-inspired, Bath's Georgian architecture and town planning were also avant-garde, radical and exciting. The new Bath was consciously engineered to support contemporary lifestyles and aspirations founded, amongst other things, on ideals of taste and the virtues of public life. In short, the city, shaped by the imagination, genius and enterprise of individuals such as Ralph Allen, John Wood (the elder) and Richard 'Beau' Nash, created a vision of the sort of place it aspired to be and then invested in its achievement.

This vision was a fusion of contemporary and classical values, social aspirations and economic ambition. It led to the creation of one of Europe's most beautiful and civilised cities, a premier spa and health resort and a celebrated 'valley of pleasure'. In addition to design, the city was equally ahead of its time in setting new standards of health-care, social behaviour and culture.

These were expressed and experienced through its grand Palladian architecture of terraces, squares, crescents and circus, its fine pump rooms and baths, its modern Mineral Water Hospital, its grand assembly rooms and theatres and, not least, within the equally impressive parades, public spaces and pleasure gardens which formed Bath's public realm.

Promenading city

A central feature and achievement in the transformation of Georgian Bath was the creation of an exceptional urban realm. This became the stage on which a vibrant and colourful public life was orchestrated: 'An agreeable urban environment mattered as much as good accommodation and the round of diversions, for the elaborate social theatre of the visitors was performed as much in the public walks and city thoroughfares as in the drawing rooms and polite assemblies. In such a fashionable resort then, attention to the arteries through which the public circulated assumed a special significance; and just as Bath found itself a trend-setter in matters of etiquette, organised entertainment or domestic architecture, so it did in the humbler sphere of street management' [2]

The city became famous for the quality of its grand spaces, promenades and parades and for the civilised social interaction and wellbeing they engendered. However such advancements in Bath's streetscape were not achieved easily and were the product of a long-term commitment, strong management and significant economic investment.

From the beginning of the 18th century, the management and maintenance of Bath's streets and public spaces was treated with increasing seriousness by the Corporation. It introduced a series of local Improvement Acts from 1707 onwards providing the necessary powers to improve, maintain and manage streets. A Board of Commissioners was subsequently established, comprising twenty of Bath's most esteemed public figures to oversee every aspect of the development and maintenance of the streetscape.

Vehicular access to the city's streets, clearly even then a source of chaos and congestion, became strictly controlled '...with even wagons of those contracted to cleanse the streets being required to have vacated the city before nine o'clock in the morning' [3] in order to create a more pleasant environment for pedestrians. This was followed by the removal of street clutter '...such as signs, boards, sheds and projections' [4] in order to tidy up the centre.

Impressive new pavements and parades of the finest pennant stone were laid and the provision of street lamps was increased, initially in principal streets, but eventually extending to all key thoroughfares.

In the interest of public safety, sentry boxes were installed (an example of which can still be seen at Norfolk Crescent), where nightwatchmen equipped with their customary staffs, rattles and lamps, stood guard.

The distinctiveness and individuality of Bath's streetscape was further enhanced by a range of delicately crafted products, many of which helped to define the boundaries between public and private space. Over two hundred years later, the enduring beauty and quality of the city's wrought iron railings, overthrows, lamps, foot-scrapers and snuffers are a testament to their original design and construction.

As the 18th century neared its end, the city's sustained programme of innovation, physical improvement and financial investment in Bath's streetscape had created one of the finest public realms in Europe and a lasting legacy for future generations. Indeed, in consciously designing, planning and managing its public streets and spaces to support the social and cultural life of its citizens and visitors, it could be claimed that Georgian Bath practically invented the concept of public realm as we know it today.

footnote
[1] and [2] from 'Paving, Lighting, Cleansing: Street Improvement and Maintenance in 18th Century Bath', Trevor Fawcett [3] and [4] from Mike Chapman et al.

Enduring qualities

As the timeline illustrates, the 18th century was a period of unparalleled creativity and productivity in the history and evolution of the city. A whole series of influences converged to refashion and reorder the physical identity, social status and economic competitiveness of Bath, creating an acknowledged masterpiece among European cities.

The development of the city's public realm was central to this achievement. It stitched together old and new parts of a radically expanded centre creating the sense of a total composition and providing a unique platform for animation, public life, pleasure and wellbeing. This achievement was underpinned by new standards of design, city centre management and maintenance which resulted in the control of vehicular traffic, the removal of street clutter and the installation of high quality and highly distinctive street furniture and finishes.

This exemplar provides a valuable and useful precedent for 21st century Bath as it embarks on the most significant period of change and growth since the Georgian era.

below
Timeline illustrating the development of Bath's public realm

1000

PEOPLE AND EVENTS		800 BC King Bladud, legendary founder of Bath and the sacred temple of Aqua Sullis		
TECHNOLOGY AND INNOVATION				
ARCHITECTURE AND URBAN DEVELOPMENT		1st C BC Vitruvius, roman writer, architect and engineer. Most famous for asserting the three qualities of furnitas (strong/ durable), utilitas (useful), and venustas (beautiful)	118–25 AD Pantheon, best-preserved Roman building and one of the oldest important building in the world	10th Century AD Bath Abbey, which had been obliterated by Norse invaders, was revived as a community of Benedictine monks living by the hot springs
THE BUILDING OF BATH		8000 BC Archaeological evidence of human activity around the springs up to 10,000 years old	70 AD The Romans commence a series of Baths and a temple dedicated to Sulis Minerva	675 The saxon name **Hat Bathu** meaning hot baths is first recorded
TRANSPORT				
STREETS AND SPACES				
STREET FURNITURE				

Travel time from Bath to London: 10 days

1500 ———— 1600 ———— 1650

1558 Elizabeth I
start of reign

1603 James I
start of reign

1625 Charles I
start of reign

1649 Oliver
Cromwell,
Lord Protector,
succeeded by
Richard Cromwell
in 1658

1660 Charles II
start of reign

1685 James II
start of reign

1090 John de Villula
began to build a new
cathedral, including
two new baths within
its precincts

1174 St John's
Hospital,
founded for the
sustenance of
pilgrims, poor
people, nuns
and monks

1508–1580
Andrea Palladio, one
of the most influential
architects of the
western world

1575–1652
Inigo Jones, regarded
as the first significant
English architect.
Influenced by Palladio
and Vitruvius

1635
Queens House,
Greenwich,
completed by
Inigo Jones

1674–1762
Beau Nash, celebrated
dandy and leader of
fashion. He played
a leading role in making
Bath the most
fashionable resort in
18th Century England

1106 King's Bath
built within the
grounds of the
monastery

1693–1764
Ralph Allen, a major
businessman and
philanthropist and a
key figure in the creation
of Georgian Bath. He
devised a scheme for
improving the postal
system and achieved a
near monopoly in the
supply and export of
Bath stone, enabling
Bath to expand into a
major spa resort

1615 Appointment
of official scavenger
or waste collector

1650s Street
lighting limited
to oil lanterns
affixed to private
buildings

The timeline outlines a range of influences on Bath's evolution as a city, including important people and events, technology and innovation, architecture and urban development, key phases of building growth, as well as specific innovations in transport, streets and spaces and street furniture. This demonstrates a fascinating convergence of influences and activities during the 18th century, which gave rise to the remarkable physical structure and form of the Georgian city. Bath peaked during this era in terms of expressing its individuality, distinctiveness and quality, which in turn strengthened its reputation and success as an international destination.

left
South Parade, c.1784

Travel time from Bath to London: 10 hours

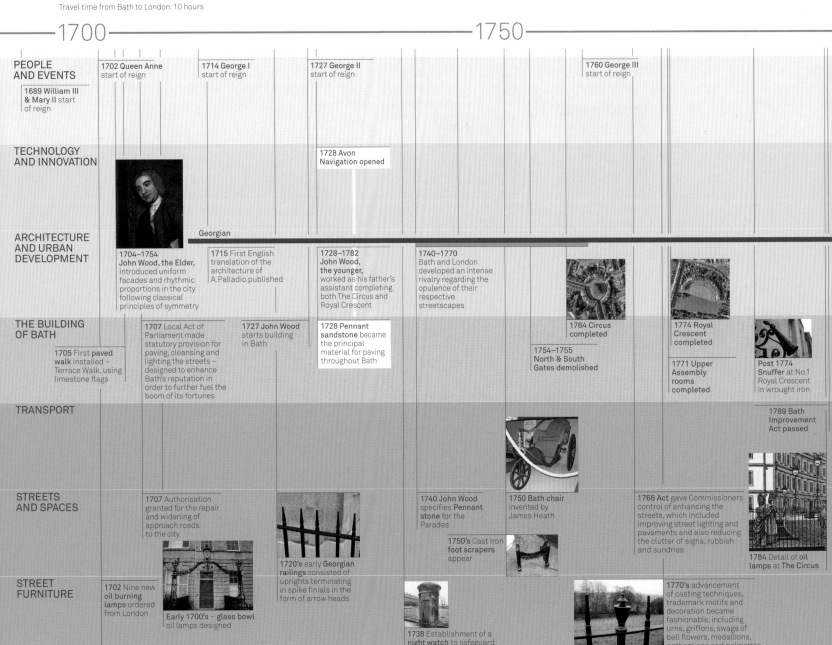

——— 1700 ——————————————————————————— 1750 ———

PEOPLE AND EVENTS

1689 William III & Mary II start of reign

1702 Queen Anne start of reign

1714 George I start of reign

1727 George II start of reign

1760 George III start of reign

TECHNOLOGY AND INNOVATION

1728 Avon Navigation opened

ARCHITECTURE AND URBAN DEVELOPMENT

Georgian

1704–1754 John Wood, the Elder, introduced uniform facades and rhythmic proportions in the city following classical principles of symmetry

1715 First English translation of the architecture of A.Palladio published

1728–1782 John Wood, the younger, worked as his father's assistant completing both The Circus and Royal Crescent

1740–1770 Bath and London developed an intense rivalry regarding the opulence of their respective streetscapes

THE BUILDING OF BATH

1705 First paved walk installed – Terrace Walk, using limestone flags

1707 Local Act of Parliament made statutory provision for paving, cleansing and lighting the streets – designed to enhance Bath's reputation in order to further fuel the boom of its fortunes

1727 John Wood starts building in Bath

1728 Pennant sandstone became the principal material for paving throughout Bath

1764 Circus completed

1754–1755 North & South Gates demolished

1774 Royal Crescent completed

1771 Upper Assembly rooms completed

Post 1774 Snuffer at No.1 Royal Crescent in wrought iron

TRANSPORT

1789 Bath Improvement Act passed

STREETS AND SPACES

1707 Authorisation granted for the repair and widening of approach roads to the city

1720's early Georgian railings consisted of uprights terminating in spike finials in the form of arrow heads

1740 John Wood specifies Pennant stone for the Parades

1750 Bath chair invented by James Heath

1750's Cast Iron foot scrapers appear

1766 Act gave Commissioners control of enhancing the streets, which included improving street lighting and pavements and also reducing the clutter of signs, rubbish and sundries

1784 Detail of oil lamps at The Circus

STREET FURNITURE

1702 Nine new oil burning lamps ordered from London

Early 1700's – glass bowl oil lamps designed

1738 Establishment of a night watch to safeguard individuals and property

1770's advancement of casting techniques, trademark motifs and decoration became fashionable, including urns, griffons, swags of bell flowers, medallions, anthemions and palmettes

Subsequent centuries saw further innovations such as the introduction of the railways, electric street lights and the Bath tram system, but the increasing dominance of the motor car during the 20th century and decades of under-investment in the public realm has resulted in a more fragmented and disconnected city centre which has lost much of the individuality, distinctiveness and quality Bath formerly enjoyed.

Travel time from Bath to London: three hours

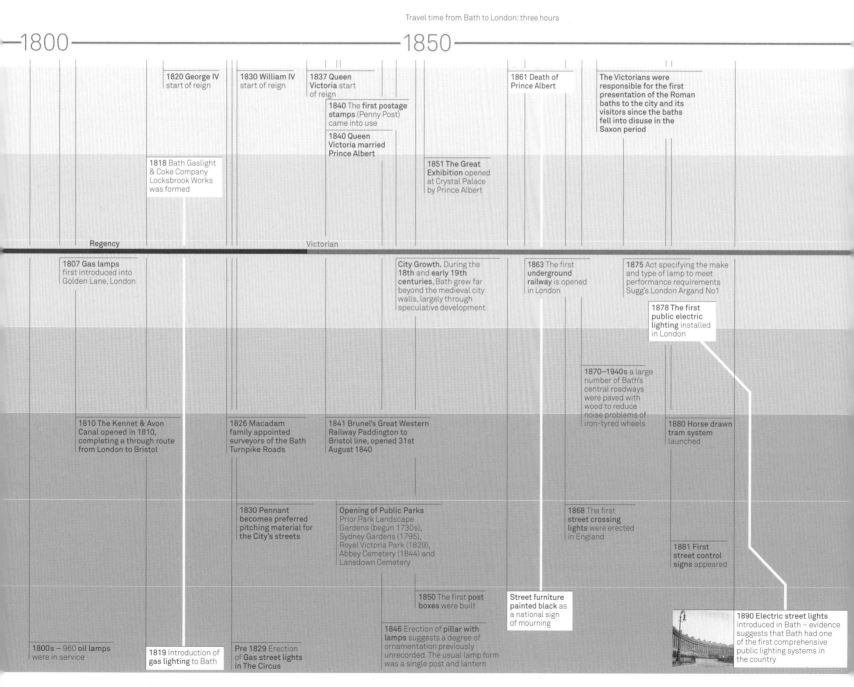

-1800 ——————————————————————— 1850 ———————————————————

1820 George IV start of reign

1830 William IV start of reign

1837 Queen Victoria start of reign

1840 The **first postage stamps** (Penny Post) came into use

1840 Queen Victoria married Prince Albert

1861 Death of Prince Albert

The Victorians were responsible for the first presentation of the Roman baths to the city and its visitors since the baths fell into disuse in the Saxon period

1818 Bath Gaslight & Coke Company Locksbrook Works was formed

1851 **The Great Exhibition** opened at Crystal Palace by Prince Albert

Regency   Victorian

1807 **Gas lamps** first introduced into Golden Lane, London

City Growth. During the 18th and early 19th centuries, Bath grew far beyond the medieval city walls, largely through speculative development

1863 The first **underground railway** is opened in London

1875 Act specifying the make and type of lamp to meet performance requirements Sugg's London Argand No1

1878 **The first public electric lighting** installed in London

1870–1940s a large number of Bath's central roadways were paved with wood to reduce noise problems of iron-tyred wheels

1810 The Kennet & Avon Canal opened in 1810, completing a through route from London to Bristol

1826 Macadam family appointed surveyors of the Bath Turnpike Roads

1841 Brunel's Great Western Railway Paddington to Bristol line, opened 31st August 1840

1880 Horse drawn tram system launched

1830 Pennant becomes preferred pitching material for the City's streets

Opening of Public Parks
Prior Park Landscape Gardens (begun 1730s), Sydney Gardens (1795), Royal Victoria Park (1829), Abbey Cemetery (1844) and Lansdown Cemetery

1868 The first **street crossing lights** were erected in England

1881 **First street control signs** appeared

1850 The first **post boxes** were built

Street furniture painted black as a national sign of mourning

1846 Erection of **pillar with lamps** suggests a degree of ornamentation previously unrecorded. The usual lamp form was a single post and lantern

1800s – 960 oil lamps were in service

1819 Introduction of **gas lighting** to Bath

Pre 1829 Erection of **Gas street lights** in The Circus

1890 **Electric street lights** introduced in Bath – evidence suggests that Bath had one of the first comprehensive public lighting systems in the country

far left
Southgate Street c.1925

left
Bath Street c.1950

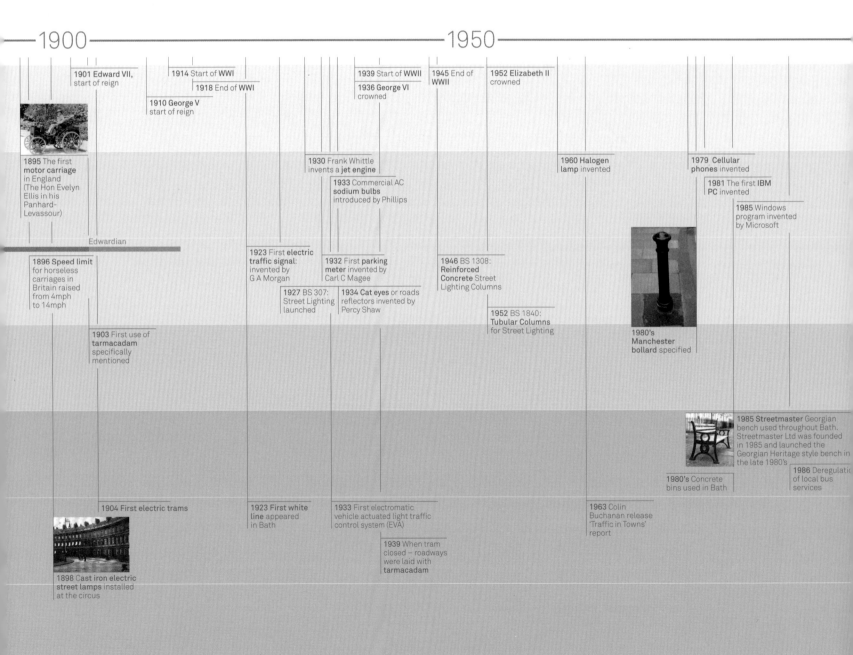

—1900—————————————————————1950——

1901 Edward VII, start of reign

1914 Start of WWI

1918 End of WWI

1910 George V start of reign

1939 Start of WWII

1936 George VI crowned

1945 End of WWII

1952 Elizabeth II crowned

1895 The first motor carriage in England (The Hon Evelyn Ellis in his Panhard-Levassour)

1930 Frank Whittle invents a jet engine

1933 Commercial AC sodium bulbs introduced by Phillips

1960 Halogen lamp invented

1979 Cellular phones invented

1981 The first IBM PC invented

1985 Windows program invented by Microsoft

Edwardian

1923 First electric traffic signal: invented by G A Morgan

1932 First parking meter invented by Carl C Magee

1946 BS 1308: Reinforced Concrete Street Lighting Columns

1896 Speed limit for horseless carriages in Britain raised from 4mph to 14mph

1927 BS 307: Street Lighting launched

1934 Cat eyes or roads reflectors invented by Percy Shaw

1952 BS 1840: Tubular Columns for Street Lighting

1980's Manchester bollard specified

1903 First use of tarmacadam specifically mentioned

1985 Streetmaster Georgian bench used throughout Bath. Streetmaster Ltd was founded in 1985 and launched the Georgian Heritage style bench in the late 1980's

1986 Deregulation of local bus services

1980's Concrete bins used in Bath

1904 First electric trams

1923 First white line appeared in Bath

1933 First electromatic vehicle actuated light traffic control system (EVA)

1963 Colin Buchanan release 'Traffic in Towns' report

1939 When tram closed – roadways were laid with tarmacadam

1898 Cast iron electric street lamps installed at the circus

Travel time from Bath to London: One hour, 15 minutes

2000 —— 2010

1987 City of Bath inscribed as a UNESCO World Heritage Site

PEOPLE AND EVENTS

1990 The World Wide Web created by Tim Berners-Lee

TECHNOLOGY AND INNOVATION

2006 Millennium technology prize awarded to **Shuji Nakamura** for work with **blue laser**

2006 Thermae Bath Spa opens

ARCHITECTURE AND URBAN DEVELOPMENT

1995 Kingsmead Square public realm enhancments commenced

THE BUILDING OF BATH

2001 Milson street redevelopment completed

2006 Traffic Regulation

TRANSPORT

1986 Opening of Bath's first Park and Ride

1990's Plastic bins begin to appear in Bath

STREETS AND SPACES

1990's Leander architectural heritage style 'Godalming" signage system introduced in Bath

2002 iplus digital information points installed in Bath (now removed)

2005 Cast iron lights recast and installed at the circus

STREET FURNITURE

2004 Bath bollard recast for use in Milson Street

THE OPPORTUNITY
REINFORCING
BATH'S DNA

The remarkable success and enduring quality of Bath's 18th century reinvention suggests that the current opportunity to refashion the public realm and movement systems within the city centre should, similarly, be guided by a clear set of values and aspirations.

Reinforcing Bath's DNA

The remarkable success and enduring quality of Bath's 18th century reinvention suggests that the current opportunity to refashion the public realm and movement systems within the city centre should, similarly, be guided by a clear set of values and aspirations. The values recommended by this strategy for Bath's 21st century transformation are, similarly, a fusion of past and future, classical and cutting edge. They are inspired by Bath's DNA and character and by the outstanding universal values of the World Heritage Site.

The values draw upon the classical ideals of order, balance, elegance, proportion and coherence and the Vitruvian principles of Utilitas (usefulness), Firmitas (durability) and Venustas (beauty). However, they also look ahead and speak of the sort of modern, vibrant, sustainable and inclusive living city that Bath aspires to become and encourage ideas and design solutions that are ahead of their time.

Overarching principles

Building on this approach, three overarching principles are recommended below to inspire the design of an exceptional 21st century public realm and to promote a distinctive visual identity for Bath:

1. Sense of place or 'Bathness'

The approach to designing Bath's public realm and movement systems should be informed by and contribute to the DNA or 'Bathness' of Bath as a place. 'Bathness' is an attempt to define the unique and special qualities of the city that make it feel like nowhere else. In a physical sense these range from natural features such as its topography, quality of light, green vistas, honey-coloured limestone and steaming hot springs; to built features such as its continuity of form, architectural set pieces, grand and intimate spaces, the relationship of built form to landscape setting and thermal baths; to quirky details such as its street names incised on buildings and 18th century wrought iron work. However, 'Bathness' also refers to a range of non-physical features which speak of the soul and spirit of the city and its people. These are articulated in more depth within the Future for Bath's DNA themes of: water and wellbeing; pleasure and culture; imagination and design; knowledge and invention; and living heritage.

2. Distinctive design

The essence of Bath and its unique attributes should infuse the design of all elements of the public realm and movement systems within the city, creating products and spaces that are distinctive and authentic to Bath. This approach strongly advocates contemporary bespoke design solutions which express and reflect 'Bathness', rather than standard 'off the shelf' solutions which speak of 'anytown'.

This distinctive design approach is recommended for a variety of products including street furniture, street signage and wayfinding systems, street market stalls, public transport vehicles and graphic and branding materials. To be successful it will require strong design direction and management and effective community engagement. In particular, it must ensure that individual design components form part of a coherent design strategy for the city centre as a whole.

3. Quality
The investment made in quality products and materials during the transformation of Bath's public realm in the 18th century is still evident on the streets of the city today. Looking ahead, it is proposed that only the highest quality of design, materials, production and maintenance should be employed for the 21st century refashioning of Bath's public realm and movement systems, reflecting Bath's status as a World Heritage Site and international visitor destination.

right
Values for Bath's transformation

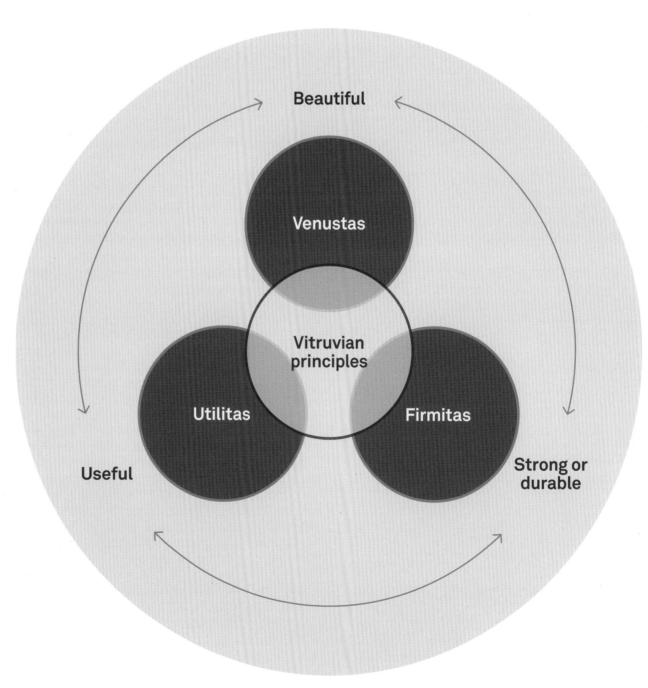

THE OPPORTUNITY
THE ESSENCE OF BATH

The application of clearly defined values at each stage of the design process will help to instil the essence of 'Bathness' in a wide range of products and services.

DNA Values

The application of clearly defined values at each stage of the design process will help to instil the essence of 'Bathness' in a wide range of products and services.

This approach has the potential to positively influence every aspect of the user experience of the city centre, helping to create a strong visual identity, point of differentiation and long term competitive advantage for Bath as a city.

The DNA values diagram (see right) provides a framework and checklist of design values to guide the refashioning of Bath's urban environment. These values provide a marker or point of reference for each stage of the design process. The diagram takes the generic values established in the Future for Bath vision, highlighting Water and Wellbeing as the most distinctive and defining theme, and then cascades these through to a matrix of Place Values and Public Realm Values and Attributes.

Of the Public Realm Values and Attributes listed there are three that warrant particular attention.

Walkable city

Bath was the UK's pre-eminent walking and promenading city in the 18th century and has the potential to achieve the same status in the 21st century. The compact nature of the city centre, its unique land ownership pattern (where large parts of the centre lie in the hands of relatively few landowners, including the Council) and its World Heritage Site status all favour a bold and innovative approach, where old hierarchies of car and pedestrian are reversed, giving people, cyclists and public transport priority access. The aspiration to make Bath the UK's most walkable city should be a central tenet of movement planning and public realm design for the entire city centre.

Total composition

As in the 18th century, Bath city centre largely continues to be read as a complete entity or total composition with important visual and physical links to the wider landscape. This applies to its buildings which, although a mixture of architectural styles from different eras, are unified by their skin of golden oolitic limestone. It also once applied to the public realm, where the streets, spaces, parks and gardens of the centre were unified by a streetscape of exceptional quality. The opportunity to reinforce a sense of total composition in a refashioned and expanded city centre should be a lodestar of the design process. However, unity should not be confused with uniformity and the simple, coherent approach recommended by this strategy must also create opportunities for individuality, variety, eccentricity and exuberance in carefully selected locations.

Lightness of touch

A key element of Bath's beauty is the lightness of touch employed in the design of the 18th century city. This applied to the simplicity and quality of the Georgian streetscape and its delicate wrought iron detailing, as well as to the elegant building facades. Today, as the public realm within the centre becomes increasingly cluttered and incoherent the adage 'less is more' suggests the way forward in terms of future design approach. Bath's streets and spaces need to be pared-back to provide a simple, beautiful, high quality setting for its breathtaking buildings and vistas. Where street furniture, wayfinding products, artworks and water features are introduced, they should be designed with a lightness of touch, a fineness of detail and structure, which are worthy of their remarkable setting.

The opportunity to reinforce Bath's DNA through the refurbishment of Bath's public realm and the rebalancing of movement systems represents a significant design and financial challenge for the city. However, successfully executed over time and combined with Bath's many other assets, it will lead to the creation of an incomparable city. It will signal the beginning of a new era in the evolution of Bath as a place where past ideals of public life, health, wellbeing and happiness are expressed in a contemporary context and are accessible to all.

Generic values

Water and wellbeing

Pleasure and culture

Imagination and design

Knowledge and invention

Place values

Style
_graceful
_avant-garde
_sophisticated
_cultured

Individuality
_unique rather than corporate
_independent spirit
_local rather than global

Beauty
_symmetry
_proportion
_balance/harmony
_elegance
_constantly reviving/rejuvenating/regenerative

Authenticity
_genuine
_distinctive
_craftsmanship
_sustainable

Public realm values and attributes

Walkable city
legible/compact/connected

Social interaction
life enabling, animation, play

Generosity of space
for pedestrian movement

Total composition
city form 'read as one'

Set pieces
an organising framework

Sequencing
continuous spaces/vistas

Formality/informality
meshing formal/informal

Blending
landscape/settings

Re-connecting
connecting/surfacing water

Lightness of touch
less is more

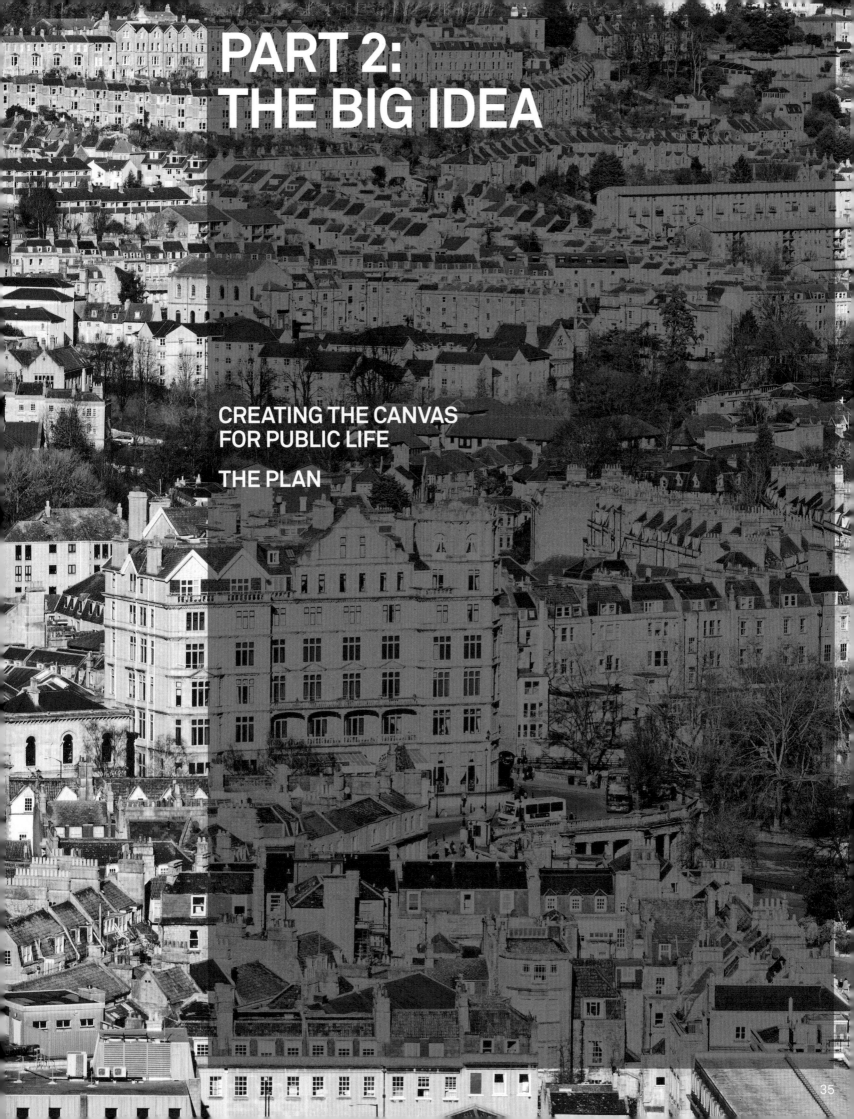

PART 2:
THE BIG IDEA

CREATING THE CANVAS
FOR PUBLIC LIFE

THE PLAN

CREATING THE CANVAS FOR PUBLIC LIFE

The canvas should be beautiful, simple, functional and coherent. It should offer diverse and well connected spaces which enable a variety of events and activities to occur. It must offer clear, coordinated information and heritage interpretation to its users and be easy to access and navigate on foot, by bicycle and by public transport.

Creating the canvas for public life

The vision and philosophy behind the Public Realm and Movement Strategy is both simple and profound. It advocates that Bath's public realm – the shared spaces between buildings in the centre of the city – should be recognised, invested-in and managed as one of the city's most valuable and exciting assets.

Bath's spaces and streets are the public rooms and corridors of the city centre, which are animated by the movement and interaction of people. The character, quality and vibrancy of these spaces has a direct influence on how local residents, visitors and businesses experience and feel about Bath and, consequently, on the image, vitality, economic success and health of the city as a whole.

Forthcoming and future measures to calm and manage the movement of vehicular traffic within the city provide a major opportunity to transform Bath's public realm into a world-class canvas for public life.

A sequence of beautiful, simple, functional and well-connected city centre streets and spaces are proposed as the basis of the canvas. These should be enhanced by sustainably sourced, high quality local materials and by unique products of exceptional design, reinforcing Bath's unique identity. This approach is not recommended merely to beautify the centre, but as part of a strategy to distinguish and differentiate Bath from other cities and to create the best possible conditions to enable a vibrant and successful public life to flourish.

Public life and wellbeing

If realised, the canvas will provide an exemplary base onto which new ideas, aspirations and expressions of public life can be added, increasing opportunities for a rich mix of people of all ages and backgrounds – residents, workers and visitors – to assemble, interact and play.

Cities have always been places for people to meet and connect and it is widely recognised that positive human interaction has the power to enhance lives, enabling higher levels of social cohesion, happiness and wellbeing. As a city which once enjoyed an international reputation as a health and pleasure resort, Bath once more has the opportunity to reinvent itself as a 21st century exemplar of urban living and wellbeing.

Walkable city

This strategy provides a long-term plan to enable Bath to achieve an international status for its public realm.

right
Plaza Oriente, Madrid

The strategy has the potential to transform Bath into the UK's most pedestrian-friendly city, reducing traffic congestion and air pollution. In addition, it will improve public information and the presentation of the city's heritage. It will allow Bath to promote its ecology with the rediscovery and enhancement of the riverside. In short, it will create the conditions for a welcoming, inclusive and engaging public life in the improved public spaces of the city centre.

When combined with the Council's Climate Change agenda and with emerging proposals for business growth, retail and culture, the Public Realm and Movement Strategy will help to redefine Bath as a leading healthy, ethical and sustainable 21st century city. It will also be a major contributor to a revitalised local economy and to a diverse, compelling and contemporary cultural life, to which people, ideas and investment are likely to gravitate.

THE PLAN
A FRAMEWORK FOR TRANSFORMING BATH'S PUBLIC REALM AND MOVEMENT SYSTEMS

Until now, the city has lacked a big picture that expresses the type of public realm and public life it is seeking to generate.

Transforming Bath's public realm and movement system over the next 20 years
The Plan is the physical manifestation of the Big Idea outlined in the previous section. It is bold and aspirational, providing a coherent long-term master plan and design framework for the transformation of Bath's public realm and movement systems. It is also pragmatic and opportunistic, advocating a long-term delivery strategy that can be implemented in phases over the next 10 to 20 years as new development and investment opportunities and public transport infrastructure are realised.

The development of the Plan provides a renewed sense of direction and potential for the future of the city centre, which is inspired by an understanding and appreciation of its past. The Plan establishes an ambitious end goal to guide and shape individual development and public realm improvement schemes within the centre so, like pieces of a jigsaw puzzle, they incrementally contribute to the fulfilment of an overall picture: in this case a unified, connected and refashioned public realm, where the whole is greater than the sum of the parts.

Delivering the Plan
It is proposed that the Plan will be implemented over the long term as part of a phased and carefully managed programme of initiatives. Each phase will contribute to the gradual transformation of the city's public realm and must be underpinned by a robust movement framework. Like any masterplan, the Plan is designed to be flexible. Changes to the proposed phasing will inevitably occur as unexpected development opportunities arise. These can be accommodated subject to the necessary transport and movement infrastructure being in place.

Bath of the future

The Plan looks 20 years ahead to a rejuvenated city centre that is perceived as a total composition. It has well-managed and maintained streets and spaces which are free of unnecessary clutter and display a sense of simplicity and order. The coherence and distinctiveness of the city centre are reinforced by a high quality range of bespoke street furniture and by the use of one type of natural stone paving throughout.

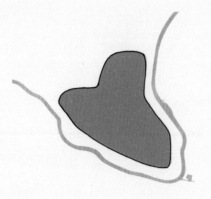

The heart of the centre is predominantly car-free and is served by an integrated access and movement system providing state of the art public transport and cycling facilities and a comprehensive range of wayfinding and information products to assist pedestrians to navigate around and beyond the centre with ease. These systems have been developed using the same design concept and values adopted for street furniture and add to an overall sense of design quality and cohesion. The centre offers a diverse range of cultural and community events and activities, public art and water features, places to eat, drink and socialise, and places for peace and contemplation.

There is a rhythm to the network of spaces and an expanded set of clear pedestrian circuits that encourage wider circulation within the city centre, supporting retail and cultural activity; and beyond the centre supporting a wider network of heritage and cultural attractions, parks and gardens, and connecting to surrounding residential neighbourhoods.

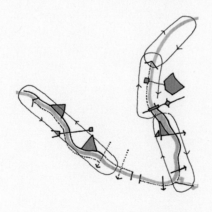

The River Corridor is a key element of the experience of the city. It offers continuous pedestrian access, a series of new and existing pedestrian bridge crossings and a variety of well-connected river corridor spaces and character areas which contribute to the green infrastructure and ecology of the city and offer a range of leisure opportunities.

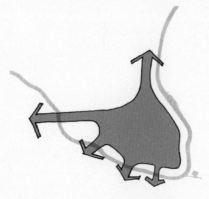

The historic core of the city centre is seamlessly connected to new development areas immediately to the East, South and West, uniting old and new architecture. Improved connections are also provided to the areas of outstanding 18th century architecture and urban design to the North and East.

The lattice

At the macro level, the Plan provides a simple mental map of an expanded city centre. This comprises a lattice of refashioned North–South and East–West streets and spaces, framed by the River Avon and an enhanced river corridor. The lattice reflects and extends the existing urban structure of the city centre.

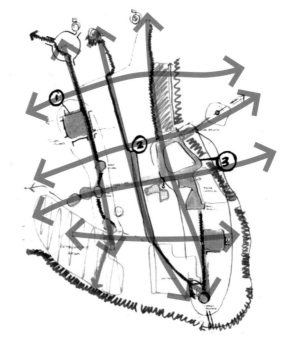

The Plan

▓ Major streets, squares and spaces to be improved

▬▬▬ Major and minor connecting routes to be improved

─── Existing routes

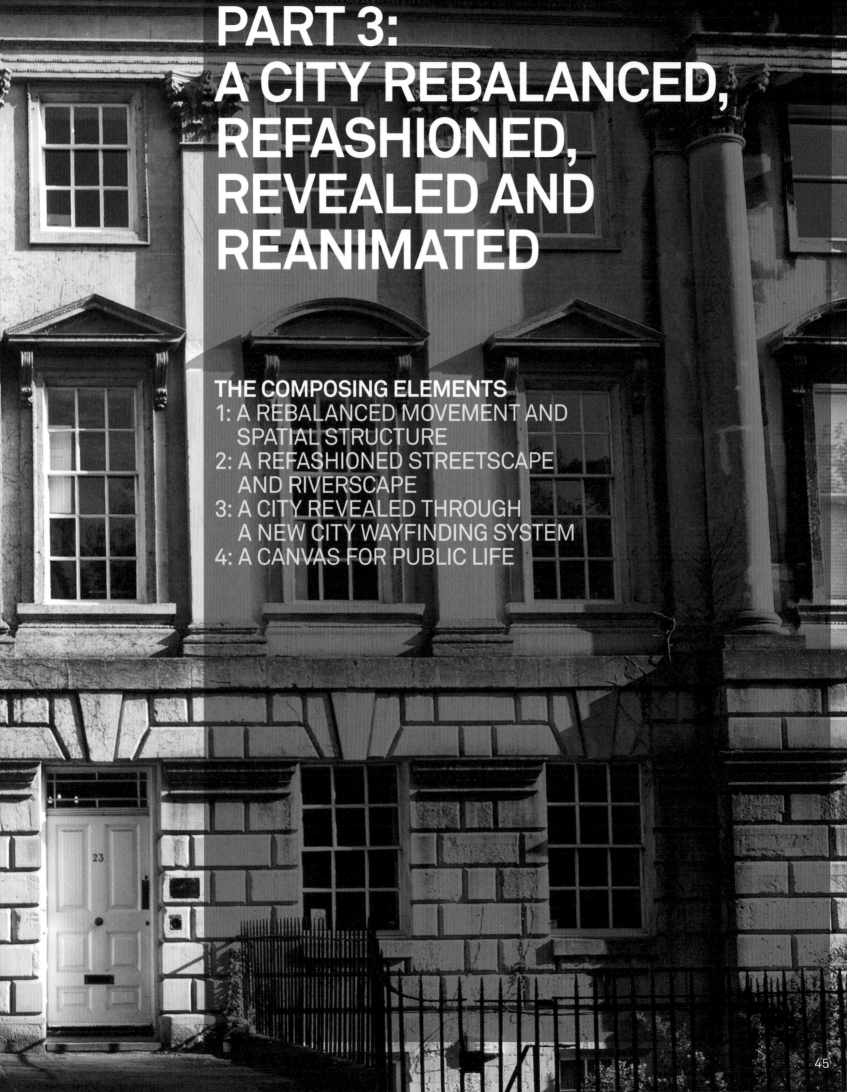

PART 3:
A CITY REBALANCED, REFASHIONED, REVEALED AND REANIMATED

THE COMPOSING ELEMENTS
1: A REBALANCED MOVEMENT AND
   SPATIAL STRUCTURE
2: A REFASHIONED STREETSCAPE
   AND RIVERSCAPE
3: A CITY REVEALED THROUGH
   A NEW CITY WAYFINDING SYSTEM
4: A CANVAS FOR PUBLIC LIFE

THE COMPOSING ELEMENTS

The approach represents a major opportunity to enhance the identity and economic success of the city and the happiness and wellbeing of its residents, workers and visitors.

Creating the canvas for public life
In order to deliver the aspirations of this strategy, a more fundamental understanding and rebalancing of the city's urban structure is required.

Like many other places, Bath's urban structure is made up of a series of interwoven layers representing different features and functions of the city. These layers include its movement and transport systems, the structure, scale and sequence of its streets and spaces, and the quality, finish and feel of the place. All of these layers can positively or negatively affect the sensory and emotional experience of using or visiting the city.

The delivery of the Plan for refashioning the public realm requires a planned programme of actions to improve each interconnecting layer of the urban structure, in order to deliver an integrated and coherent city centre, which provides an outstanding canvas for public life.

This holistic approach to integrating movement, connecting streets and spaces and revealing and refashioning the place as part of one coherent plan is unusual and forward-thinking. It represents a major opportunity to enhance the identity and economic success of the city and the happiness, health and wellbeing of its residents, workers and visitors. However, it will require a step change in the existing management of the city, requiring strong, intelligent leadership and coordinated, collaborative and multidisciplinary working within the Council and across a range of sectors in order to ensure that each component contributes towards the delivery of the total composition.

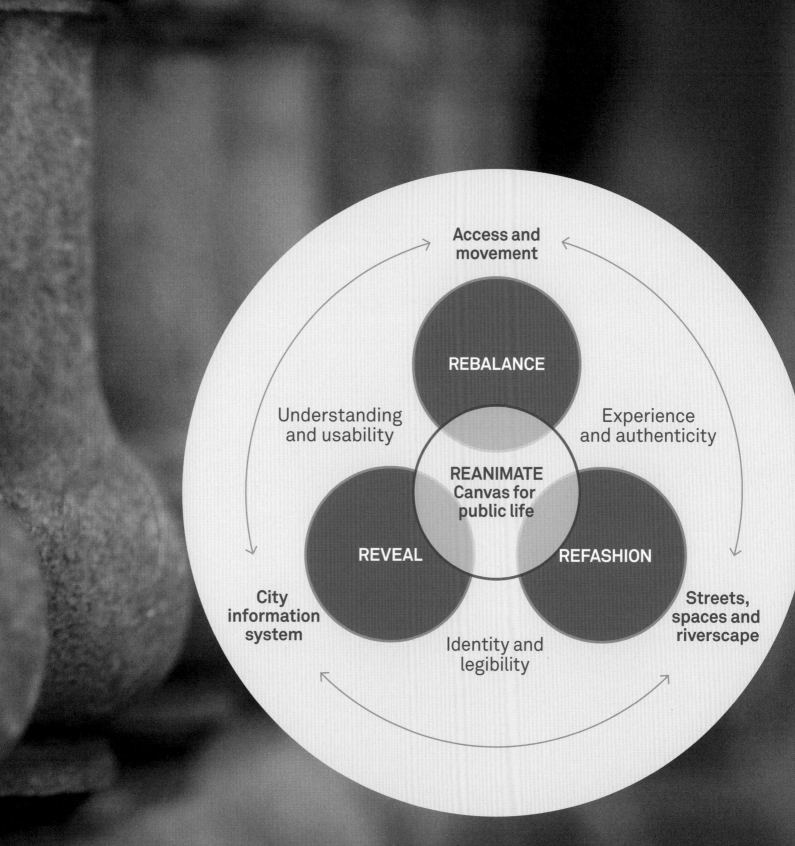

Access and
movement

REBALANCE

Understanding
and usability

Experience
and authenticity

REANIMATE
Canvas for
public life

REVEAL

REFASHION

City
information
system

Streets,
spaces and
riverscape

Identity and
legibility

1. Rebalancing Bath's movement and spatial structure

Access and movement within the city is naturally complex and challenging, but a rebalancing of the existing movement and spatial structure is required in order to achieve an expanded pedestrian-friendly city centre. This layer contains a description of the range of interconnected traffic and movement issues from the local to the regional, and proposes a series of measures that seek to rebalance and improve levels of accessibility into and around the city.

The majority of these actions are already planned and most are contained within The Joint Local Transport Plan for the West of England. Some of these actions require additional research and development, while others already have funding identified and are planned to be implemented.

This approach is not anti-car and acknowledges the important role that cars will continue to play in modern life and in the future of Bath's economy.

However, it advocates that intelligent and innovative solutions are required to re-order access and movement priorities within the city centre in order to put pedestrians, especially the mobility impaired, then cyclists and public transport vehicles firmly at the top of the movement hierarchy. This is essential to enable Bath to create better, healthier and more enjoyable places for people.

New proposals and solutions for the city centre must also acknowledge the importance of securing and improving access for people whose mobility is impaired.

2. Refashioning Bath's streetscape and riverscape

This layer addresses the network of streets and spaces within the city centre, and the connections to the River Corridor environment, parks and open spaces and surrounding residential neighbourhoods. It seeks to overcome the challenge of decline and decay within the public realm over recent decades and to establish a lattice

reanimate *verb* /ree'animayt/

restore to life, restore to activity or liveliness

reveal *verb* /ri'veel/

display or show, allow to appear

refashion *verb* /ree'fash(ə)n/

fashion again or differently

rebalance *verb* /ree'bal(ə)ns/

balance again, restore the correct balance to

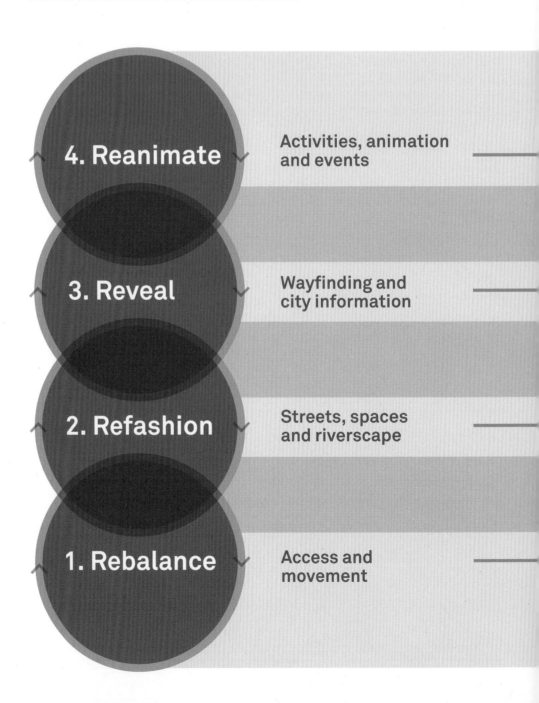

4. Reanimate — Activities, animation and events

3. Reveal — Wayfinding and city information

2. Refashion — Streets, spaces and riverscape

1. Rebalance — Access and movement

of beautiful and successful destination spaces across an expanded city centre and along a rediscovered River Corridor. These spaces, which will be refashioned or designed to offer a variety of atmospheres, activities and events, will be well-connected by civilised pedestrian-friendly streets, encouraging people to explore and experience a larger area of the centre and wider city beyond.

It also proposes a new, contemporary bespoke range of street furniture for the city centre and the resurfacing of streets and spaces with natural stone paving.

3. Revealing Bath through a new wayfinding and city information system

This layer recognises the important role information plays in ensuring the city is easy to access and enjoyable to live, work and relax in. It will ensure an information interface is developed for Bath that makes day-to-day journeys to and around the city easier and more efficient, whilst also attracting more visitors to spend time in the city's spaces and destinations. It proposes a whole journey approach, that will link and connect information across all channels of delivery at all stages of the journey. The system will balance simple, hierarchical information with highly detailed mapping and interpretation to meet the users needs and successfully communicate the city.

4. Reanimating Bath's centre through activities and events

The previous three layers will, in combination, help to create a canvas for public life in Bath over the next 10 to 20 years that could result in a renaissance of urban living, cultural expression, economic success, environmental sustainability and health and wellbeing for the city's residents, businesses and visitors.

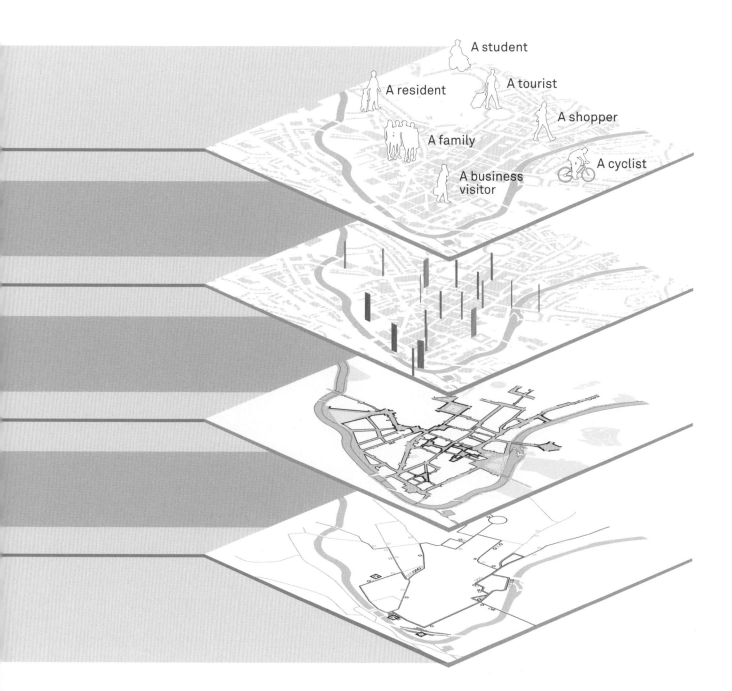

left
The composing elements

1: A REBALANCED MOVEMENT AND SPATIAL STRUCTURE

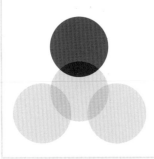

The primary objective is to reorder and rebalance transport and movement systems within the city in favour of the pedestrian, cyclist and public transport user. This approach provides the key to unlocking and reclaiming a network of connected streets and spaces and promoting the canvas for public life.

Key issues

The tension between the movement of vehicular traffic and pedestrians within the city centre is referred to under The Decline of the Public Realm in Part 1, Page 12. Large areas of Bath city centre currently feel as though they have been designed for cars and not people.

The primary objective is to build on and influence current and future plans to reorder and rebalance transport and movement systems within the city in favour of the pedestrian, cyclist and public transport user. This approach provides the key to unlocking and reclaiming the network of connected streets and spaces and to stimulate the vibrant public life aspired to in Creating the Canvas for Public Life.

There are already some successful fully or partially pedestrianised streets and spaces within the centre such as the central shopping spine of Union Street to Southgate Street and the public spaces around the Abbey and Roman Baths. In these areas public life is able to flourish, to such an extent that it results in high levels of overcrowding at peak times.

A range of other measures have been introduced over the past 30 years, including restrictions to East–West vehicular through movement across the city centre.

More recently, the introduction of the Priority Access Point – commonly referred to as the Bus Gate – which limits North–South routes, has removed significant levels of through traffic from the centre reducing congestion in some central streets, and improving the experience for pedestrians.

It is on the more peripheral streets and spaces adjacent to the city core that the impact of congestion, particularly for pedestrians, is most problematic. The environmental quality currently experienced in parts of the city centre is frequently compromised by near constant vehicular movement through a significant number of streets and spaces including George Street, Queen Square, and in front of Green Park Station. This constrains the heart of the city centre, providing a barrier to the delivery of an expanded centre, generates high levels of air and noise pollution, and impedes the free flow of pedestrians.

Initial modelling exercises of city centre traffic movement have identified opportunities to change the balance of certain city streets and spaces in favour of the pedestrian. Some of these proposals will have a minimal impact on highway capacity by enabling traffic to be reasonably accommodated elsewhere within the network. However some proposals will have an impact on capacity and will require the provision of suitable alternatives before they can be realised.

Unlocking the potential of the city centre

The successful movement of people into and within the city is highly dependent on an integrated approach with the wider region and the city's broadest catchment area. Convenient access from major cities such as Bristol and areas of significant population such as the Midlands, South Wales and London as well as from key arrival points such as Bristol International Airport, are crucial to ensure a successful future for the city. Local towns within the district such as Keynsham, Midsomer Norton and Radstock and a number of neighbouring Wiltshire and Somerset towns look to Bath as a major centre for employment, shopping, and culture. The city needs to continue to ensure easy access for its catchment area if it is to sustain its appeal and economy.

At peak times, Bath's key radial routes are at the limits of their capacity. With nationally forecast growth in vehicular traffic, and with anticipated levels of development, it is essential that current and future transportation challenges are proactively addressed. Without bold new movement solutions and changes in behaviour – particularly the habitual use of cars for short, local journeys – the city is unlikely to fulfil many of the aspirations of the Council's vision and its appeal as a visitor, shopping and business destination will decline over time.

Measures are required to maintain convenient access to the city whilst also reducing the penetration of private cars into its pedestrian heart. Any proposed improvements to the movement network should take into consideration the likely impacts upon the Strategic Road Network (SRN), namely the A4, A36, A46 and M4. Proposals to remove or restrain private car access in the city centre should be supported by the provision of alternative methods of transport, to minimise the impact of shifting the private car elsewhere.

Currently there is a high perception of Park and Ride services, however, perceptions of other forms of alternative transport need to be improved significantly. Public transport must be more frequent, reliable, affordable and appealing. Cycling should be encouraged with enhancements to the cycling network. Above all, the city centre must become more civilised to encourage people to swap their cars for other modes of movement.

CONGESTION IN BATH

Annual cost of congestion in Bath = £50m (Joint Local Transport Plan).

21% of travelling time in the Bath, Bristol, North Somerset and South Gloucestershire region is spent at a standstill.

Bath's road network is severely constrained.

Over 27,000 people drive to work in the city every day, and a third of these are Bath residents. There is an average car occupancy rate of 1.1 persons per car.

Public transport is adversely affected by congestion.

Congestion creates pollution.

Pedestrians and vehicles compete for limited space in the city.

The Government states 8,000 new homes have to be built in Bath, including the urban extension. This is forecast to result in increased commuting by car.

Exceedances of National Air Quality Objectives for hourly mean concentrations of nitrogen dioxide in numerous locations.

The movement strategy

Over the next 20 years the West of England sub region is set to respond to the requirements of growth set out in the Regional Spatial Strategy. Growth targets for Bath and North East Somerset are being addressed through the development of the Core Strategy and Local Development Framework. The levels of anticipated growth are significant and an efficient transport infrastructure is essential to enable this scale of development to be realised.

This challenge has been recognised initially within the Joint Local Transport Plan to 2011 developed with North Somerset; Bristol City and South Gloucestershire Council. This plan contains comprehensive multi-model proposals and solutions which have been formulated through a rigorous consultative process. They address the wide range of issues that affect Bath and other areas within the region and are grouped under the main national objectives of:

_tackling congestion
_improving road safety for all users
_improving air quality
_improving accessibility
_improving the quality of life

Measures contained in the Joint Local Transport Plan form part of the Council's Capital Programme for transport and include a range of current initiatives and projects that will provide the basis for rebalancing Bath's movement and spatial structure.

First generation projects

Key transport initiatives include The Greater Bristol Bus Network (GBBN), The Bath Package and the EC CIVITAS programme.

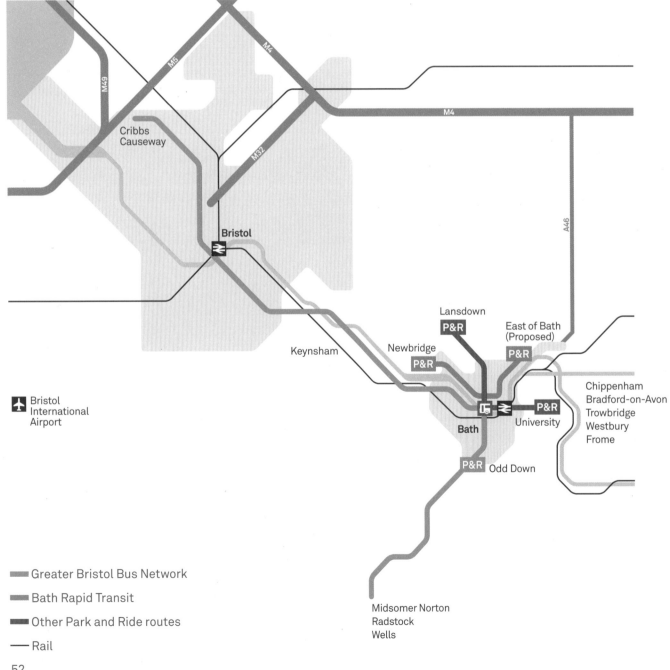

left
Bath and its regional connections

Cribbs Causeway

Bristol

Lansdown
P&R

East of Bath (Proposed)
P&R

Newbridge
P&R

Keynsham

Bristol International Airport

Chippenham
Bradford-on-Avon
Trowbridge
Westbury
Frome

P&R

Bath   University

P&R   Odd Down

Midsomer Norton
Radstock
Wells

M49
M5
M4
M32
M4
A46

■ Greater Bristol Bus Network

■ Bath Rapid Transit

■ Other Park and Ride routes

— Rail

First generation projects

Greater Bristol Bus Network

The GBBN is an initiative that has £42 million of Government funding. It will benefit people through the introduction of showcase bus routes that will significantly improve levels of bus based access to the city. Work is currently in progress to upgrade strategic bus routes into Bath and Bristol from surrounding areas by 2012. Key features of the initiative:

The X39, 173, 178 and 184 bus routes will be upgraded to showcase status. This is anticipated to increase bus patronage by implementing a significant enhancement to the quality of service provided.

The bus routes will include dedicated buses, 'real time' information systems and bus stop infrastructure.

The Bath Transportation Package

The Bath Transportation Package (BTP) is a £54 million scheme designed to tackle congestion in Bath and the surrounding area by improving public transport and enhancing pedestrian access for the benefit of residents, commuters and visitors. The BTP includes the following elements:

Expanding the city's three existing Park and Rides and creating a new Park and Ride to the East of the city, thereby increasing Park and Ride capacity from 1,990 to 4,510 spaces.

Creating a Bus Rapid Transit (BRT) route, including a 1.4km section of "off-street" dedicated bus route which will remove Park and Ride buses from congestion for a significant amount of their journey.

Creating a more pedestrian and cyclist-friendly city centre through the introduction of access changes on a number of streets and the expansion and enhancement of pedestrian areas.

Improving nine bus routes to Showcase standard, including raised kerbs for better access, off-bus ticketing to speed up boarding and real-time electronic information for passengers.

Introducing active traffic management with real-time information to direct drivers to locations where parking spaces are available.

The BTP formed the basis of a Major Scheme Business Case (MSBC) bid to the Department for Transport in 2006. 'Programme Entry' for the BTP was confirmed in October 2007, meaning that Government funding for the scheme was provisionally secured through its Major Transport Scheme funding process.

The BTP will be complemented by other initiatives that will be delivered as part of the development of the SouthGate area at the Southern edge of the city centre. These include:

A new public transport interchange including a revamped Bath Spa Station and new bus station at SouthGate, linked by a new public space.

A remodelled Dorchester Street, aimed at enhancing this key gateway and welcome point to the city, reducing the impact and volume of parked buses, and improving pedestrian movement across the space.

CIVITAS Renaissance

The Council has secured €4 million of European Commission (EC) funding to improve transport options in Bath. With the Council's own contribution and funding from partners, the total project will invest £5.15 million into the city. The programme will explore innovations in transportation and implement research and pilot projects that push existing boundaries. The programme will complement the BTP bid by ensuring that design quality and innovation are embedded within the proposals. Key features of the programme:

A feasibility study into a personal rapid transit system for the city centre.

The implementation of initial phases of a new user-focused wayfinding and public transport information system for the city.

The implementation of a freight transhipment depot outside the city to manage deliveries into the centre, thereby reducing the number of delivery vehicles required to enter the city centre.

Trial clean fuel technology for public transport.

The introduction of an electronic/ automatic bike hire system for the city including powered bicycles.

An expansion of the City Car Club including the trialling of hybrid vehicles.

The 'first generation' initiatives of the GBBN, Bath Package and CIVITAS outlined above will bring levels of Government, EC and private sector partnership funding that are unprecedented in Bath's recent history. They represent a major step forward in the provision of public transport and new technology and will play a major part in rebalancing access and movement within the city over the next 20 years, assisting the delivery of key parts of the Plan for a refashioned public realm.

Bristol
Keynsham

Midsomer Norton
Radstock

left
The Greater Bristol
Bus Network in Bath's
city centre

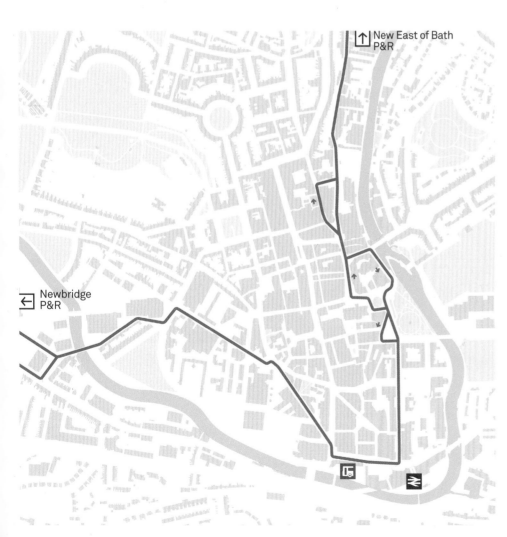

New East of Bath
P&R

Newbridge
P&R

left
Bath Rapid Transit
route in Bath's
city centre

below
Proposed transport
connections

Second generation projects

To enable a more radical refashioning of
Bath's public realm a second generation
of movement and access measures
are proposed to achieve the long term
aspirations of this strategy and to build on
the improvements already described above.
These measures are recommended to be
included in the next 15 year Local Transport
Plan to 2026. They include a range of enabling
strategies and research projects that will
provide the framework to develop major
public realm projects. They are based on
the emerging Government policy objectives
for future Local Transport Plans:

_productivity and competitiveness
_climate change
_safety, security and health
_quality of life including environment
_equality of opportunity

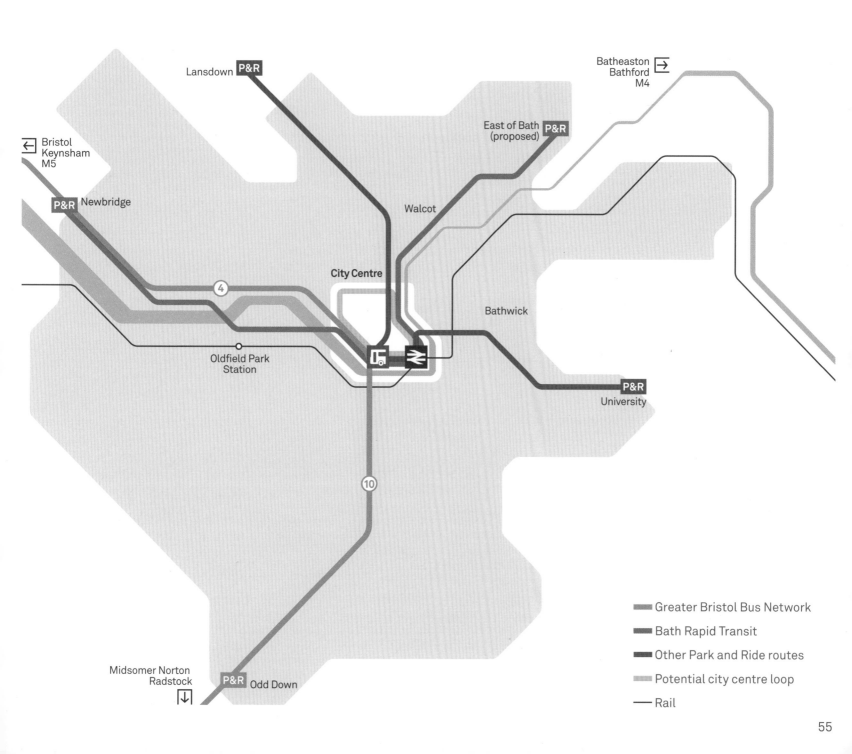

Legend:
- Greater Bristol Bus Network
- Bath Rapid Transit
- Other Park and Ride routes
- Potential city centre loop
- Rail

Productivity and competitiveness

1. In response to the Government's Transport Innovation Fund (TIF), work is underway to assess the viability and benefits of submitting a major scheme bid for demand management in the West of England sub region, including Bath.

2. The regional funding allocation agreed by government currently identifies a scheme for the A36/A46 link road post 2016. Any proposals for this link would have to take into account the impact on the World Heritage Site landscape setting and other environmental impacts. A study of HGV movements in Bath is in progress following the government's decision not to proceed with the A350 Westbury Bypass (in Wiltshire) which could have provided an alternative route for HGVs travelling between Bristol/ South Wales and Dorset.

3. Proposed study into the relocation of the coach park to enable the redevelopment of Bath Quays North (the area that includes Avon Street car park and the existing coach stations). New facilities could be located on one site or spread through different parts of the city. Options include a reconfiguration of Charlotte Street Car Park, using a part of the Cricket Club site or coach storage at park and ride sites or other peripheral areas of the city. Implement enhancements for drop off provision for coaches including increasing number and variety of drop-off points over a wider area of the centre.

4. Network Rail intends to upgrade signals on the main rail line running through the city to increase rail capacity in 2010. Its Route Utilisation Strategy makes recommendations for other rail service improvements within the current infrastructure.

Climate change

1. The potential for 10–20mph zones to make the city centre safer for pedestrians and cyclists.

2. Encouragement and expansion of the car club and car share concept, in particular through the statutory planning process (obligations and consents).

3. The implementation of a local and strategic cycle route network in and around the city centre, connecting neighbourhoods, and developing the potential of cycling as an alternative mode of transport including promoting the benefits of cycling as a healthy, convenient and non-polluting mode of transport and increased public information on practicalities of cycling to continue the upward trend in cycle use. It is recommended that this could be preceded by the implementation of a pilot project focussed on improving one key cycle route between a local neighbourhood and the city centre.

4. A similar pilot project could also be developed to improve key walking routes between local neighbourhoods and the city centre.

Safety, security and health

1. Strategy to develop and implement proposals to reduce air pollution on all of the main routes through the city which are now designated as Air Quality Management Areas (AQMA), as many of them suffer from pollution levels that are higher than legal limits. The designation of an AQMA requires the local authority to devise an Action Plan to reduce levels of pollution. The introduction of cleaner emission vehicles is occurring as a result of national or European legislation and improvements in engine technology. Further local transport improvement measures relating to emissions are also under consideration as part of the Air Quality Plan for Bath. The plan is being drafted in close collaboration with the EC CIVITAS project and Bath Transport Package

Quality of life including environment

1. Ensure any new Parking Strategy for Bath city centre addresses the multitude of issues associated with existing demand and with projected growth of residential, retail, hotel and business development within the centre which could increase demand and displace existing car park sites. The Parking Strategy would also need to consider the better use of Park and Ride facilities, provision of overnight parking for hotel guests and the process for re-provision and reallocation of on street car parking spaces displaced by projects proposed through this strategy.

2. Proposed bus network planning and capacity study and research into increasing the frequency of the wider bus network, with improved vehicles and user-focused design quality, such as integrating cycle carrying facilities and on-street ticketing.

3. Feasibility studies towards the implementation of a more integrated and expanded Bus Rapid Transit System including city centre mini interchanges that integrate BRT, Park and Ride and Showcase bus stops.

By aligning the routing of services and stops, the aim will be to reinforce a simplified public transport network, aid interchange between one service and another and reduce on street clutter of furniture and bus stops.

4. Investigate the potential of a circular transport route around the city core.

5. Working with partners, commission the design of a new Bath bus/vehicle of outstanding contemporary design and of appropriate scale for the centre of a heritage city, that utilises the latest hybrid/green technologies developed through the CIVITAS proposals.

6. Ensure the continued provision of a delivery transhipment facility for the city improving the problems associated with deliveries in the city centre. Working with partners to extend the initial pilot proposals developed through CIVITAS.

7. Investigate potential changes to taxis to lower emissions and the provision of cycle carrying facilities.

Equality of opportunity

1. Feasibility and design study to develop a typology/range of streetscape measures based on a hierarchy of streets and spaces including further pedestrianisation, shared spaces, widening pavements and reducing street clutter.

2. Feasibility and design study to explore the closure of up to three sides of Queen Square. This would radically change the perception of one of the city's most beautiful and important spaces, bringing it back into the daily life of the city by relieving the almost constant flow of traffic and the impact of on-street parking. More significant changes are dependent upon the implementation of strategic measures such as the A36/A46 link road. Such proposals have the potential to create more radical opportunities such as the complete removal of through traffic from George Street and Queen Square, a long term aspiration of this strategy.

3. Feasibility and design study leading to the closure of Pulteney Bridge to buses and taxis. This would improve a currently constrained and dangerous pedestrian space and build better connections to Argyle Street, Great Pulteney Street, the Holburne Museum and Sydney Gardens.

4. Experimental closure of Milsom Street to vehicular traffic, initially for one day a week, enhancing the ambience and pedestrian experience of this shopping environment.

5. Implementation of safe city centre storage facilities for shopping, coupled with timed deliveries to home or Park and Ride sites.

6. Proposed study to improve the provision of facilities for the mobility impaired through the extension of shopmobility schemes integrated with arrival points such as car parks, bus and train services.

right
It is proposed that a feasibility study be undertaken to examine the scope for revising the city centre bus route network. The study will explore the potential to integrate an expanded BRT system including city centre mini interchanges that integrate BRT, Park and Ride and Showcase bus stops, to potentially form a public transport loop. By aligning the routing of services and stops, the aim will be to reinforce a simplified public transport network, and aid interchange between one service and another. The loop could form the perimeter of a city centre 20mph zone. Speed limits in certain streets within this zone could be further restricted to five or 10mph.

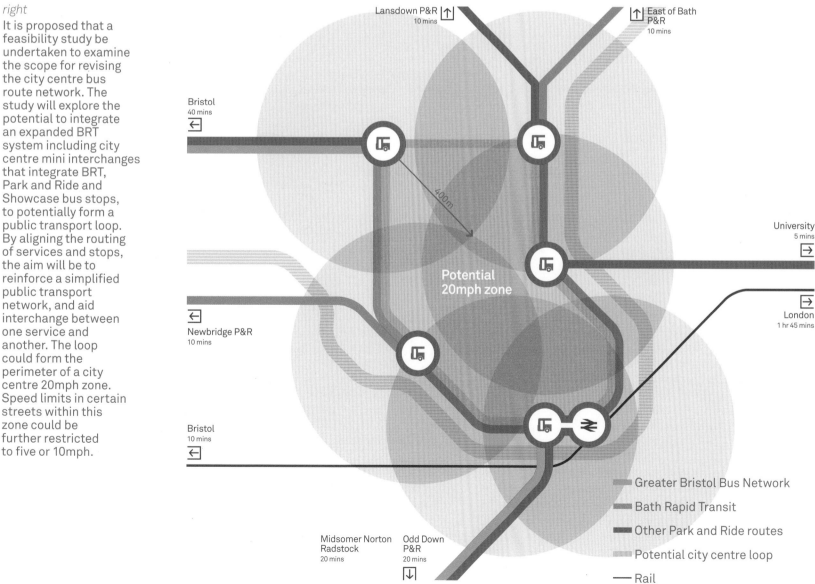

Lansdown P&R
10 mins

East of Bath
P&R
10 mins

Bristol
40 mins

400m

Potential
20mph zone

University
5 mins

London
1 hr 45 mins

Newbridge P&R
10 mins

Bristol
10 mins

Midsomer Norton
Radstock
20 mins

Odd Down
P&R
20 mins

Greater Bristol Bus Network

Bath Rapid Transit

Other Park and Ride routes

Potential city centre loop

Rail

2: A REFASHIONED STREETSCAPE AND RIVERSCAPE

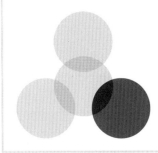

This section focuses on the streets and spaces between Bath's buildings, the river and its surrounding environment and the city's green spaces, all of which need to be connected and refashioned to create a canvas for public life.

Key issues

As outlined in Part 1, Page 22, 18th century Bath was a national and international exemplar of city design, with its streets and spaces laid out to create and encourage social and cultural interaction. Buildings and the spaces between were designed as a total ensemble, providing ideal pre-conditions for public life and allowing open or glimpsed views of the city's sublime landscape setting.

However, the legacy that we have now inherited has become degraded. While the basic urban structure of much of the city is still largely intact, its integrity as a total ensemble has been eroded. The qualities of many of the city's streets and spaces now contrast with rather than complement the qualities of its buildings. The key issues relating to Bath's streets, spaces, parks, gardens, riverscape and landscape setting are as follows.

Streets and spaces. Many of Bath's streets and spaces are currently laid out for and dominated by vehicular traffic, rather than for social and cultural interaction. Tarmac as a material tends to define key routes and many footways are paved in poor quality and poorly maintained materials. The proliferation of signage and an uncoordinated range of street furniture further compound the experience of a city that now falls a long way short of the design values prevalent in its heyday, and of its current World Heritage Site status.

Parks and gardens. Interspersed within the dense network of Bath's buildings, streets and spaces are a number of attractive and important parks and green open spaces. These 'green lungs' provide contrast and relief to the harder urban core of the city centre and each green space offers a different environment and experience for the user. Some parks such as Royal Victoria Park are central to the life of the city centre, hosting major events while others are much more local in significance or are hidden oases; one such example is Henrietta Park, which, while located within a five minute walk of the city centre, is mainly frequented by local residents or those in the know.

The River. Although the shape and size of Bath's city centre is, in part, defined by the meandering course of the River Avon, its once beautiful river is given little prominence in the current life of the city. The river should be seen as one of Bath's greatest natural assets.

Many streets such as Westgate Street and large parts of Stall Street are still laid out for vehicular movement rather than reflecting their dominant use by pedestrians.

Pavements are often too narrow for the numbers of pedestrians using them resulting in people stepping into busy roads to pass others.

Existing street surfaces and narrow pavements restrict the ability of cafés and restaurants to put tables and chairs on pavements, undermining the potential for café culture.

Poor quality, uncoordinated and broken concrete paving materials are a common sight throughout much of the city centre.

Pedestrians are encouraged to cross at formal crossing points rather than following natural lines, reinforcing the sense that large parts of the centre are designed for cars and not people.

There is a plethora of uncoordinated signs, posts and bollards in many parts of the city, detracting from the beauty of buildings and from townscape views and occupying valuable pedestrian space.

Street furniture is dated, of poor quality and often poorly maintained.

Pedestrian and vehicular signage and mapping is difficult to understand and lacks a coherent and consistent design language.

The river is a neglected asset currently providing limited pedestrian access and in parts is an ugly and poorly-maintained environment.

Sadly, with the exception of the small area around Pulteney Bridge and Weir, it currently contributes little to the experience of Bath's public realm. The Georgian city, for reasons principally of health and sanitation, largely turned its back on the river and this approach continued and was compounded during Bath's 19th and 20th century industrial expansion.

Recurrent flooding became an increasing problem within the city centre and in the 1960's and 1970's a range of successful flood prevention measures were implemented along the river.

While these measures continue to be effective, it is widely acknowledged that a number of the features installed, such as long stretches of sheet piling and the sluice gate at Pulteney Weir, have been detrimental to the visual appearance and appeal of the river within the centre.

Large parts of the River Avon offer good pedestrian access, while in other parts access is limited or completely obstructed.

The 18th century legacy of Bath turning its back on the river continues and even recent developments such as the new SouthGate retail scheme and transport interchange, conform to this tradition. The public realm along the river is often ugly and neglected and does little to promote the attractiveness of Bath as an international visitor destination and World Heritage Site. Nevertheless, despite these challenges and constraints, the River Avon continues to provide a major amenity to the city, loved and appreciated by many.

Landscape setting. Bath's dramatic landscape setting is integral to the beauty of the place and to its identity as a World Heritage Site. It contains the city, providing a visual reminder of its boundaries and an enticing connection to the open countryside beyond. Fingers of green woodland, open farmland or grassland descend from the valley sides well into the city, contrasting with and softening the buildings.

The city's 18th century townscape was consciously designed to sit within and respond to this landscape.

Buildings were often located to frame vistas of wooded hillsides and open fields and public spaces to exploit and enjoy the views. Today this relationship between the city and its surrounding landscape remains largely intact and must continue to be valued as an inherent feature of the city and an essential backdrop to its public realm. Interventions within and around the city will need to protect and enhance the outstanding universal values of the World Heritage Site, such as the emerging World Heritage Site setting assessment.

The future of Bath's surrounding woodland requires better understanding and management, if it is to continue to provide a visual and environmental asset for the city. Much of the existing tree stock is mature and a programme of tree replenishment needs to start now to avoid a decline in the quality of the wooded hillsides in 20–30 years time. There is also a need for tree surveys and an enhanced woodland management regime to maintain and improve the tree cover surrounding the city and to implement a phased tree planting programme in partnership with land owners such as Bath and North East Somerset Council and the National Trust. There are opportunities here to establish a tree fund, to which residents and businesses could contribute, to finance such a programme.

As well as playing a significant role in defining Bath's landscape setting, trees also make a major contribution to the character of its streets and spaces, the quality of life of its people and the biodiversity of the city as whole. Trees connect people to nature and offer shelter and comfort. They provide cleaner air at a time of increasing air pollution, as well as shading and cooling. Public realm enhancements will provide opportunities to contribute to the green infrastructure of the city as well as actively reducing flood risk.

The arrangement of trees in Bath's public realm is characterised by single mature specimens as in Abbey Green or Kingsmead Square, or groups of trees in spaces such as in The Circus. Trees in key spaces within the city provide important contrast to the built form as well as visual interest.

There are opportunities for new tree planting within the proposals to refurbish the city's streets and spaces. However, these need to be carefully measured to ensure that the city's townscape characteristics are enhanced rather than eroded.

right
River Avon, Bath

The streets, spaces and riverscape strategy

This strategy recommends a comprehensive refashioning of Bath's streets, spaces (including parks and gardens) and river setting, using high quality natural landscaping materials, beautifully designed street furniture, atmospheric lighting and contemporary public art to provide richness and sensory interest and to enhance the historic fabric.

It seeks to create an interconnected network or 'lattice' of pedestrian-friendly streets and spaces, as outlined in the Plan in Part 2, Page 40, stimulating and creating new levels of activity within the public realm and in building frontages. This new structure will reveal and extend the experience of the city centre for its users and provide the pre-conditions to realise the Big Idea outlined in Part 2, Page 35.

The pedestrian-friendly network will seamlessly connect a variety of streets and public spaces which are capable of hosting different types of activity (organised and informal) at different times. Where vehicular movement is permitted, new levels of control and management of access are proposed (including temporary road closures to facilitate activities within city streets eg. street markets, sports events and festivals), complemented by the new transport measures.

The production of a Bath Pattern Book, a constantly evolving design resource, is recommended to provide clear standards and specifications on the treatment of the city's streets and spaces responding to the design values of the city and its important historic context. It will define the siting, design, materials, quality of workmanship and quantity of the complete range of elements within the public realm. More details on the proposed Bath Pattern Book are provided in Part 4 The Design Elements, Page 103.

Key spatial sequences

Whilst the Bath Pattern Book will be underpinned by a cohesive approach to design which seeks to establish a more unified city centre by using natural stone paving and a contemporary range of bespoke street furniture, it will also acknowledge that different streets and spaces may require different design solutions depending on their character, use and function. This approach presents an opportunity to emphasise, through subtle streetscape design or public art, key features of an area to reflect its particular role within the city centre. This is intended to improve its character and legibility for the benefit of users.

Some of Bath's existing spaces form the major historical set pieces of the city and combine with streets to form important spatial sequences. For example Queen Square, Gay Street, The Circus, Brock Street and Royal Crescent. In this tradition, the opportunity now exists to create new sequences within the urban structure that combine new spaces with existing ones that have been reinvigorated or reclaimed through traffic restraint measures.

As a priority, the strategy proposes the phased enhancement of the key North–South central shopping spine and associated retail circuits. Over time it is proposed to reinforce an East–West axis across the centre, as redevelopment opportunities arise and by improving a range of public spaces and streets. These improvements will help to connect a series of existing and proposed cultural attractions from Bath Western Riverside and Green Park Station, potentially via a new 'living bridge' (eg. a contemporary version of Pulteney Bridge) in the West, to the Holburne Museum of Art and Sydney Gardens to the East. These sequences will be supplemented by projects to enhance associated streets, squares and spaces, eventually building to the completion of the overall plan and a seamless walking network of streets and spaces.

Major streets and spaces
to be improved

Retail North–South sequence

(1) Saville Row and Bartlett Street
to George Street

(2) Milsom Street to
Old Bond Street
and Burton Street

(3) Union Street to Stall Street

(4) SouthGate to
Dorchester Street

Cultural West–East sequence

(5) Bath Western Riverside to
Green Park Station

(6) James Street West to
Kingsmead Square

(7) Westgate Street to Cheap Street

(8) Orange Grove and Grand Parade
to Pulteney Bridge

(9) Laura Place to Sydney Gardens

Major streets,
squares and spaces
to be improved

Major and minor
connecting routes
to be improved

Existing routes

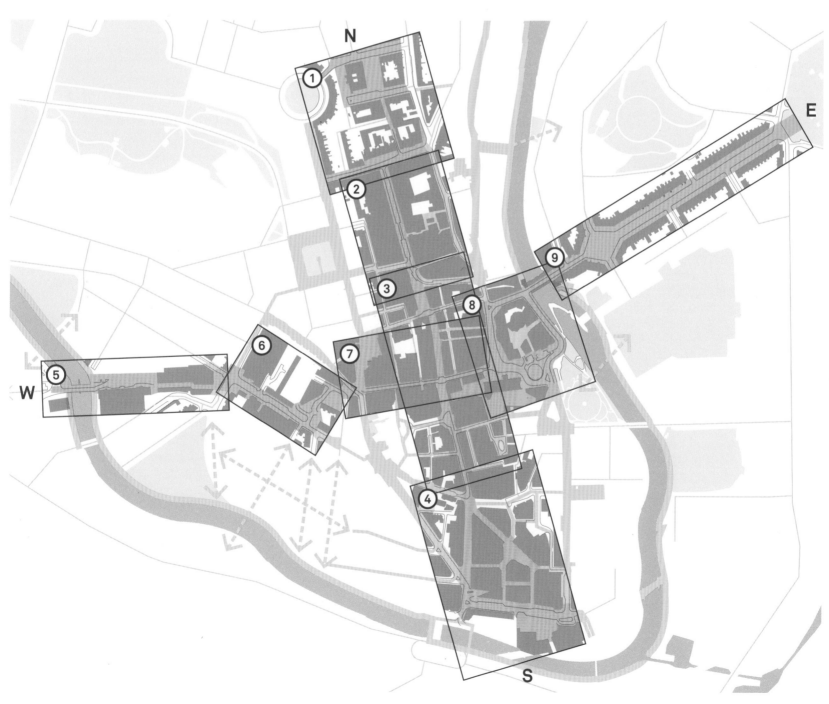

Creating the walking network – typologies of streets and spaces

The location, degree of connectivity, physical form, size, nature and extent of surrounding building uses and the need to accommodate vehicular movement are all key factors that will affect how individual streets and spaces can be used for a variety of activities and events. A clear relationship therefore exists between the function of streets and spaces and their design treatment. For example, spaces which are seen as destination and event hosting spaces will be designed differently from those which are seen as soft landscaped spaces for passive recreation.

Typologies of streets and spaces have been developed (see opposite) as a means to help inform a more detailed consideration of the range of planned and informal activity that could take place within them. This in turn will influence their design treatment. The typologies are not intended to stifle new patterns of use within streets and spaces and along the river that may arise over time. The ability of the public realm to adapt to changing circumstances, be it new public transport infrastructure or new development proposals, is fundamental to its continued attractiveness and relevance to the local community, businesses, potential investors and visitors.

An interconnecting walking network

The table (see opposite) sets out a three level pedestrian route hierarchy. City streets function as spaces for walking and as space to accommodate vehicular movement that supports the economic wellbeing of the city. The proposed hierarchy reflects a rebalancing of movement systems within the city centre to favour the pedestrian, cyclists and public transport, thereby stimulating and creating new levels of activity within the public realm and frontage buildings. Further opportunities to facilitate activities within city streets (eg. street markets, road running races and rallies) are proposed via temporary road closures.

ROUTE HIERARCHY	ROUTE FUNCTION	ROUTE FORM
LEVEL ONE **The lattice – major routes** A lattice of North–South and East–West routes that form the major connecting routes (streets and River Corridor walkways) within the city centre pedestrian route network. These streets connect points of arrival (interchanges, car parks) and all primary destinations and visitor attractions.	The lattice is composed of routes which combine the following functional characteristics related to movement and access by travel mode.	The form and appearance of the public realm along lattice routes will vary in response to the function attributed to sections of individual routes.
	Pedestrianised _Accommodating high levels of footfall (time sensitive vehicular access for deliveries, servicing and maintenance).	Pedestrianised route sections _Level paving surface no kerbs (subject to historic environment). _Surface treatment – natural stone paving. _New foot bridge crossings of the Avon River.
	Multi-use restricted local vehicular access _10–20mph zones, integrated cycle lanes where part of strategic cycle route network, blue badge holder, emergency vehicle and taxi access.	Multi-use restricted local vehicular access route sections _Footway and kerbs. _Maximum footway widths (subject to historic environment, equalities and vehicular access requirements). _Surface treatments – footway natural stone paving, carriageway – i) surface dressed or paved (street interchanges, pedestrian crossings, on street parking and loading bays, feature spaces); ii) tarmacadam. _Road markings and traffic signage to be kept to a TSRGD minimum.
	Multi-use public transport route and restricted and or managed local vehicular access _Integrated cycle lanes where part of strategic cycle route network, blue badge holder, emergency vehicle and taxi access.	Multi-use public transport route and restricted and or managed local vehicular access route sections (as above).
	Public transport and taxi access – Time sensitive vehicular access for servicing, deliveries and maintenance.	Public transport and taxi access (as above).

ROUTE HIERARCHY	ROUTE FUNCTION	ROUTE FORM
LEVEL TWO **Connecting routes** The lattice is supported by pedestrian routes which provide cross connections to and from it and which link to secondary destinations.	Cross-connecting routes provide alternative and shorter length links to and from the lattice and cross-connecting routes. They exhibit the following functional characteristics related to movement and access by travel mode:	The form and appearance of the public realm along lattice routes will vary in response to the function attributed to sections of individual routes.
	Multi-use restricted local vehicular access. _10–20mph zones, integrated cycle lanes where part of strategic cycle route network, blue badge holder, emergency vehicle and taxi access.	Multi-use restricted local vehicular access route sections. _Footway and kerbs. _Maximum footway widths (subject to historic, environment and vehicular access requirements). _Surface treatments – footway natural stone paving, carriageway – i) surface dressed or paved (street interchanges, pedestrian crossings, on street parking and loading bays, feature spaces); ii) tarmacadam. _Road markings and traffic signage to be kept to a TSRGD minimum.
	Multi-use public transport route and restricted and or managed local vehicular access. _Integrated cycle lanes where part of strategic cycle route network, blue badge holder, emergency vehicle and taxi access.	Multi-use public transport route and restricted and or managed local vehicular access route sections (as above).
	Public transport and taxi access. _Time sensitive vehicular access for servicing, deliveries and maintenance.	Public transport and taxi access (as above).

ROUTE HIERARCHY	ROUTE FUNCTION	ROUTE FORM
LEVEL THREE **Minor connecting routes** A number of street blocks within the city centre are sub-divided by pedestrian-only routes (lanes, arcades, yards passageways and alleyways). These fine grain routes contrast in length and scale to those of the lattice and cross-connecting routes but enable linkages to both. In some cases street block routes present high levels of active frontage.	Pedestrian-only routes. _Accommodating high to low levels of footfall.	Pedestrian-only routes. _Level paving surface no kerbs. _Restricted footway width in some locations. _Some routes public highway others rights of way. _Surface treatment – natural stone paving. _Limited street furniture and signing to avoid clutter.

Proposed projects – streets

The enhancement of the major routes as outlined in the above typology will create the basic lattice or skeletal structure of key pedestrian routes in the city centre. This lattice will connect the parts of the city centre that host the richest variety of activities. It is intended to strengthen existing and new retail and cultural circuits and encourage a wider dispersal of pedestrian activity. The lattice will also form the main framework for the implementation of wayfinding products and services.

The lattice will be further refined and complemented by the connecting routes, which combine to create a complete network of pedestrian-friendly streets. These connecting routes provide alternative choices that are intended to encourage greater exploration, resulting in the connection and discovery of new parts of the city centre, enriching the experience of Bath.

The connecting routes also link to destinations further afield including regeneration areas, and will help to increase footfall to lesser known areas and to various attractions dispersed across the city.

These proposals will clearly have policy and revenue implications in terms of displaced on street parking.

● North–South major streets

1 Walcot Street
2 Broad Street/ Northgate Street
3 Manvers Street
4 Milsom Street to SouthGate
5 Gay Street
6 Barton Street
7 Westgate Buildings
8 St James Parade
9 Churchill Bridge
10 Charles Street

● East–West major streets

1 George Street
2 Wood Street/Quiet Street
3 New Bond Street
4 Upper Borough Walls
5 Bridge Street
6 Great Pulteney Street
7 James Street West
8 Westgate Street/ Cheap Street
9 York Street
10 North Parade
11 Lower Borough Walls/ New Orchard Street/ Henry Street

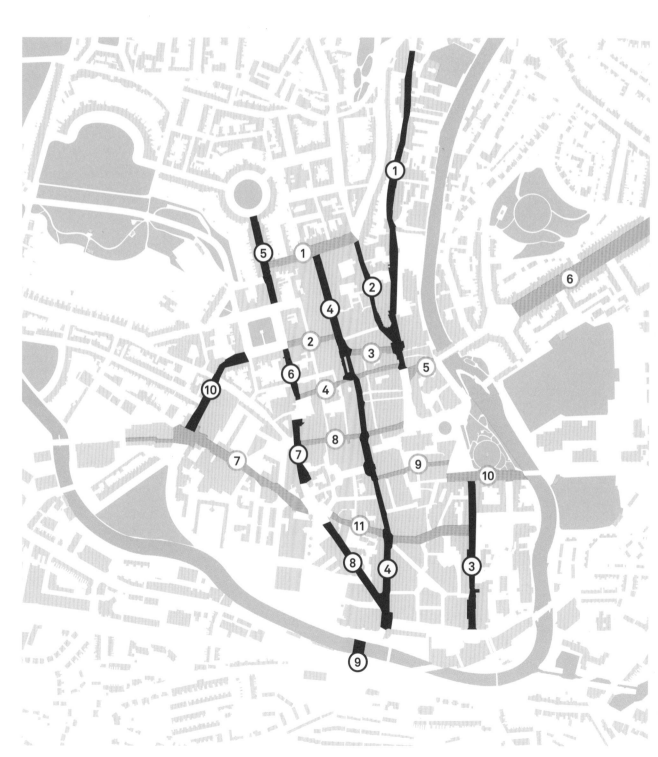

(1) Walcot Street

Renewed public realm associated with redevelopment of Cattlemarket, Hilton and Podium sites improving the linkages further up Walcot Street.

New pedestrian bridge link to Grove Street and Henrietta Park.

(2) Broad Street/Northgate Street

Widened footways paved in natural stone to enhance the pedestrian experience and reinforce its role as a retailing circuit that connects to the Podium, Walcot Street and Milsom Place and Green Street.

Traffic management restrictions to close lower half of Broad Street for large parts of the day.

(3) Manvers Street

Footway improvements using natural stone.

Restore original line of building frontages in any future redevelopment of Police Station site to reinforce street.

(4) Milsom Street to SouthGate

This major sequence of streets and spaces plays a crucial role in the economy of the city as its central shopping spine. It connects SouthGate in the South of the city to Milsom Street, via Stall Street and Union Street, to the North. Pedestrians dominate this space, yet the existing design and layout lacks any coherence or consistency throughout its length.

An enhancement of most of this area is long over due, and necessary to provide an environment conducive and appealing to the thousands of pedestrians that use this route on a daily basis. There is also an economic imperative; its poor environmental quality has been highlighted by the new public realm at SouthGate which could potentially impede the natural flow of pedestrians Northwards through the central shopping spine and affect the city's reputation as a retail destination.

It is proposed that a shared surface be created with widened footways and a carriageway laid in natural stone setts, extending the paving typology as agreed for Southgate Street. For most of the time this would be a pedestrian-only space, with controlled access for delivery vehicles within set hours.

(5) Gay Street

Forms a major connection between the set pieces of Queen Square and The Circus, but is dominated by vehicular movement which at times makes crossing the street very difficult for pedestrians particularly at the junction with George Street.

Introduction of informal crossing points to assist pedestrian movement whilst maintaining the aesthetic quality of the townscape.

Replace concrete paving on footways with natural stone.

Consider restrictions to vehicular access between corner of George Street and The Circus.

(6) Barton Street

Links Queen Square to Saw Close.

Repave and widen footways using natural stone.

Repave carriageway using natural stone setts.

Promote outdoor seating areas connected with existing restaurant and café uses.

(7) Westgate Buildings

Links Saw Close, Seven Dials and Kingsmead Square with proposed new midi public transport interchange at St James Rampire.

Restricted vehicular use to reduce pedestrian conflict at Seven Dials and minimise congestion for public transport providers.

Repave footways using natural stone.

Repave carriageway using natural stone setts if possible.

(8) St James Parade

Widen and repave footways using natural stone if possible.

(9) Churchill Bridge

A key route that connects residential areas from the South of the city centre. Enhance quality of the pedestrian route with renewed paving and where possible tree planting. Improvements to the quality of the pedestrian crossings and underpass. Identify opportunities for enhancing the relationships of buildings to adjacent public realm.

(10) Charles Street

Widen and repave footways using natural stone if possible.

Soften hostile nature of street with tree planting.

East–West major routes

1 George Street

Widen footways on the South side and repave using natural stone.

Introduce informal crossing point at junction of Gay Street and George Street.

Improve pedestrian links to the Assembly Rooms and Fashion Museum via Bartlett Street and Gay Street.

2 Wood Street/Quiet Street

Displace car parking in Wood Street.

Footway widening in Wood Street/ Quiet Street to create improved link with Milsom Street.

Encourage change of use of adjacent uses to food and drink, and use of widened footway for seating.

3 New Bond Street

Widen footways and carriageway resurfacing in New Bond Street to improve pedestrian link to The Podium and onwards.

4 Upper Borough Walls

Repaving of carriageway using natural stone.

Reconfiguration of space at the Northern end of Union Street.

5 Bridge Street

Replace concrete paving with natural stone.

6 Great Pulteney Street

Repaving of footways using natural stone.

Resurfacing of carriageway.

See proposals for Pulteney Bridge on page 74.

7 James Street West

This route forms a critical linkage from the city centre to the regeneration areas of Bath Western Riverside and Bath Quays. Its enhancement using the same palette of materials as the rest of the city centre and the introduction of bespoke street furniture would help to integrate the street into the fabric of the city.

8 Westgate Street/Cheap Street

This has the potential to become the key East–West route within the city centre strengthening the connection between Parade Gardens and Pulteney Weir to the East with Green Park Station and The River Corridor to the West. Footway widening and repaving using natural stone for footways and carriageways. Proposed new traffic management regime creates the opportunity for cafés to open onto the street. Potential for light and/or water features along the route.

9 York Street

Displace car parking.

Footway widening to create improved link between central shopping spine and Terrace Walk.

Encourage change of use of adjacent uses to food and drink, and use of widened footway for seating.

Replace concrete paving with natural stone.

New traffic management regime to facilitate time limited vehicle access to frontage properties for deliveries.

10 North Parade

A key route that connects residential areas from the East of the city centre. Widen pavement particularly on the North side, and repave using natural stone. Consider the opportunities to open up access to Parade Gardens, and improve quality of access to the River Corridor.

11 Lower Borough Walls

Important route that connects central shopping spine to proposed new midi public transport interchange at St James Rampire and the Spa complex and via New Orchard and Henry Streets to Manvers Street.

Displace car parking.

Natural stone for the footways.

Natural stone for the carriageway.

Connecting routes

A consistent approach to the treatment of all the connecting routes will complement the approach proposed for the key routes that form the lattice. This will include the phased replacement of concrete paving with natural stone, the introduction of bespoke street furniture products, and a de-cluttering programme to enhance their visual appeal. The principal connecting routes to be improved are:

North–South connecting routes
_Bartlett Street
_Charles Street
_Queen Street
_New streets within SouthGate

East–West connecting routes
_Bennett Street
_Green Street
_Saracen Street
_Trim Street
_Bath Street
_Beau Street
_Abbeygate Street
_New Orchard Street
_New streets within SouthGate
_Corn Street
_Somerset Street
_Broad Quay

Minor connecting routes

Minor connecting routes include The Corridor, Northumberland Passage, Union Passage, Bridewell Lane, St Michael's Place, Hetling Court and Bilbury Lane. They add an important level of choice for pedestrian movement throughout the city centre and many require repaving using natural stone to enhance their aesthetic qualities and appeal, and to seamlessly connect into the lattice of major routes and connecting streets.

Typology of spaces

It is proposed that the enhanced pedestrian route network outlined previously is punctuated, connected to and animated by a variety of high quality public squares and spaces that vary in scale, landscape treatment and intensity of use. This variety will enrich the city's offer and appeal, catering for the needs of a diverse range of people.

The spatial typology set out in the table below will be used to inform the enhancement and remodelling of existing spaces and the design of new spaces. The design treatment of individual spaces will also respond to a range of other factors including the form and use of surrounding buildings, orientation and topography and will be the subject of public consultation.

The proposed typology will also be used to inform the appropriate level of maintenance and management for individual spaces. It is proposed to stimulate new levels of activity and public life by remodelling spaces which are currently eroded by the detrimental and intrusive impacts of traffic or enhance existing spaces which have under-exploited potential for greater levels of public activity.

SPACE TYPE	GENERIC FUNCTIONS	GENERIC FORM QUALITIES
TYPE ONE **Arrival and departure spaces**	_Orientation. _Journey planning. _Information provision. _Onward transport modes. _Drop off/pick up. _Good first impression. _Cycle parking.	Spaces of various scales located at interchanges and major car parks; predominantly hard landscaped.
TYPE TWO **Destination squares and spaces**	_High levels of informal and passive recreation and leisure. _High levels of organised activity linked to formal events programme. _High quality facilities – children's play areas, activity areas, toilets, child and carer facilities, café (temporary kiosks or pavilion). _Electrical power/water points to support event activity. _Information and interpretation provision. _Cycle parking. _Public transport stop within 200m.	_These spaces represent the main public space assets and outdoor activity hubs of the city centre. _Major spaces located across the pedestrian route network including: Squares (hard and soft landscaped); Parks and gardens; Recreational spaces; and Riverspace. _Significant public art and water features. _Creative and amenity lighting provision. _High levels of seating. _Shade/weather protection.
TYPE THREE **Intimate spaces**	_Pause, rest/meeting point. _Public transport stop within 400m.	_Smaller scale, quieter spaces located off the lattice and cross-connecting pedestrian route network or within street blocks. _A variety of hard and soft landscape. _Shade/weather protection where context permits. _Good seating provision.

Proposed projects – spaces

The city's extensive network of spaces should be revealed and articulated as the public rooms of the city; transforming them from spaces to places – creating new city destinations. As outlined in the table above, they will offer a range of experiences and will be connected to the lattice of streets so that the user can choose or discover the different qualities that each space contains. Some spaces will be hubs of activity offering places to meet friends or be entertained by street theatre, others will be quieter, providing places to unwind and relax away from the busy pedestrian central shopping spine. Areas such as Orange Grove, Terrace Walk, Saw Close, and Queen Square are just a few of the city's spaces that could be reclaimed and refashioned as places for meeting, eating, drinking, entertainment, play and performance.

The proposed implementation of the projects is outlined in more detail in the Making it Happen section. This recommends the initial implementation of projects that are without critical dependency on transport infrastructure, and which make the most of opportunities currently presented.

Arrival and departure spaces

1. Dorchester Street
2. Railway Station Forecourt and Vaults Square
3. High Street
4. St James Rampire

Destination squares and spaces

1. Queen Square
2. Laura Place
3. Pulteney Bridge
4. Pulteney Weir, East Side
5. Grand Parade
6. Orange Grove
7. Terrace Walk
8. Manvers Street/ South Parade
9. Southgate Place
10. Abbey Churchyard and Kingston Parade
11. Saw Close
12. Kingsmead Square
13. Green Park Station/ River Corridor
14. In front of St Michael's Church

Intimate spaces

1. Corn Market Square
2. Broad Street Place
3. Rear of Guildhall
4. Abbey Green
5. Burial Ground
6. Green Park Station Forecourt

Parks, gardens and recreational spaces

1. Hedgemead Park
2. Walcot Gate Park
3. Henrietta Park
4. Sydney Gardens
5. Recreation Ground
6. Parade Gardens
7. Green Park
8. Norfolk Crescent
9. Royal Victoria Park

Arrival and departure spaces

① Dorchester Street

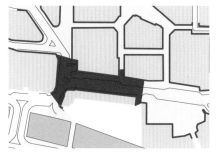

Creation of an on-street public transport interchange linked to the SouthGate scheme and the provision of a new bus station

New footways and crossing points linking bus stop areas, bus station and SouthGate development

② Railway Station Forecourt and Vaults Square

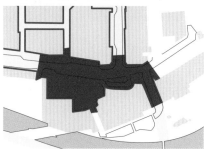

Remodelling of Railway Station forecourt to provide enhanced setting to the station and improved access for taxis and drop off and pick up.

Creation of new pedestrian space West of the station entrance acting as outdoor waiting room, connection to Dorchester Street interchange and gateway to the city centre.

Improvement to access routes.

③ High Street

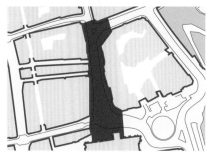

Creation of an on-street public transport interchange as a key component of the Bath Package.

Remodelling of Guildhall area to create improved and extended footways and bus stop areas/ midi interchange.

Widened footways at Orange Grove.

New traffic management regime to enable time limited access to frontage properties including set down and pick up bay to service surrounding uses.

④ St James Rampire

Creation of public space and on-street midi interchange accommodating the Bath Rapid Transit and limited bus services.

Footway improvements in Westgate Buildings and St James Parade to create high quality pedestrian link to Westgate Street/Kingsmead Square/Bath and Dorchester Street public transport interchanges.

Destination squares and spaces

① Queen Square

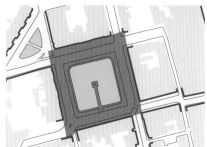

Proposal to work with owners to explore the following options:

Phased downgrading and closure to traffic of two to three sides of the square. Relocation of on street car parking spaces.

Remodelling of Queen Square to include pedestrianisation of South and East side perimeter roads.

New traffic management regime to facilitate time limited vehicle access to frontage properties.

Potential widening of perimeter and inner footways.

Improvements to inner landscaped square to facilitate limited event performance use, including potential removal of railings and coordinated lighting.

Ultimate objective to radically reduce vehicular through traffic in Queen Square. This is dependent on achieving significant reduction of vehicular traffic in the city or through a major infrastructure project to provide alternative routes.

② Laura Place

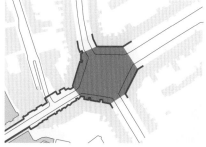

Reconfiguration of Laura Place to create shared space focus including water feature.

3 Pulteney Bridge

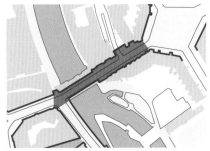

Pulteney Bridge has the potential to be traffic free. For one of the city's most famous landmarks, this creates the opportunity for a simple, high quality public realm enhancement project that is responsive to the architectural significance of the Bridge structure and which can provide a transformed environment. This could include reconstruction of the Western Pavilion of Pulteney Bridge providing access to the lower level of Grand Parade.

Extending the city centre from Pulteney Bridge to Argyle Street, thereby improving the sequence of spatial connections to Great Pulteney Street, Henrietta Gardens, The Holburne Museum, and Sydney Gardens.

Enabling activities from buildings to spill into the street, providing animation and variety of interest.

Enabling the public to better experience the architectural splendour of one of the world's few remaining living bridges.

Improving the quality of connections and access to the East side of the river.

4 Pulteney Weir, East Side

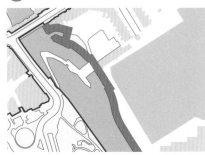

Creation of new public open space adjacent to Pulteney Weir and enhancement of promenade to North Parade Bridge.

Opportunity for al fresco dining linked to surrounding cafés and restaurants.

5 Grand Parade

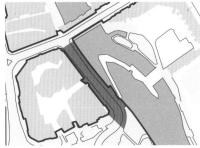

Connecting a remodelled Orange Grove to Pulteney Bridge, Grand Parade should be repaved using natural stone on footways and carriageways to provide a sublime space overlooking Pulteney Bridge, the river and the hillsides beyond. There are significant opportunities for outdoor seating associated with adjacent businesses and subject to more detailed traffic modelling, the potential of removing through traffic from this route.

6 Orange Grove

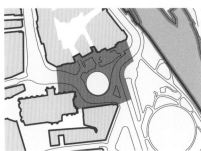

Orange Grove, once a fine grove of trees, has enormous potential to be remodelled as a key new landscaped heart of the city, connecting the tourism honey pot of the Roman Baths, Pump Room and the Abbey to Parade Gardens and The River Corridor. This would extend the offer and experience of the city centre, improving connections with the green spaces and the river; opening up development opportunities underneath Grand Parade and potentially connecting through to a new Walcot River Corridor path.

7 Terrace Walk

Remodelling to create improved setting for surrounding building frontages; extended pedestrian space linking, restored fountain feature and potential future gateway to Parade Gardens and or under-croft attractions; integration of seating; and redefined vehicle access route to York Street. Relocation of on street car parking spaces and coach drop off and pick up points. Access requirements related to hotel to be accommodated.

Reconfiguration of Terrace Walk to create public space.

Removal/rationalisation of on street car parking and tour bus stop facilities.

8 Manvers Street/South Parade

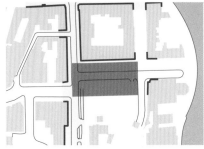

Explore the opportunity to create a new destination space or parade adjoining South Parade and in front of St John's Church as part of the proposed redevelopment of parts of Manvers Street.

Destination squares and spaces

⑨ Southgate Place

Creation of a new space as a result of the SouthGate shopping centre scheme. This mostly hard landscaped and pedestrian-only space is located at the heart of the centre on the diagonal pedestrian route linking the Railway station, Dorchester Street interchange with the Stall Street, Union Street, Milsom Street retail axis.

⑩ Abbey Churchyard and Kingston Parade

Being adjacent to the Abbey, the Roman Baths and the Pump Rooms, these spaces are host to vast numbers of tourists every year. There is a pressing need to introduce high quality bespoke street furniture into these areas and to remodel the arrangement of street furniture to create more welcoming and relaxing spaces.

Management of events and busking in these areas is required to maximise their benefit.

⑪ Saw Close

Removal of surface car parking, creation of space enclosed by the Theatre Royal, other existing frontage buildings and new development or building refurbishment. Significant potential to promote a dynamic daytime and nightime multi-use space, eg. accommodating cultural activity, markets and pavement cafés. Predominantly hard landscaped and capable of accommodating limited vehicular traffic.

New traffic management regime to facilitate time limited vehicle access to frontage properties including the Theatre Royal and Mineral Hospital.

Removal/relocation of B&NES surface car park.

⑫ Kingsmead Square

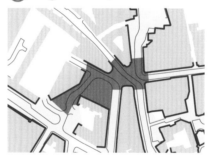

Enhancement of Kingsmead Square and Trinity Street approach including improved traffic management measures, facilities to host specialist markets, and kiosks with outdoor seating/café culture.

Street furniture and lighting improvements to Kingsmead Square.

New traffic management regime.

Rationalisation and resurfacing of vehicle access route.

Removal/rationalisation of car parking.

Footway improvements to James Street West.

⑬ Green Park Station/ River Corridor

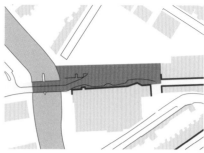

A major new destination space and new bridge proposed to connect Green Park Station (potential future use as a major market and event space) to the River Corridor as part of proposals to redevelop the Eastern end of Bath Western Riverside.

⑭ In front of St Michael's Church

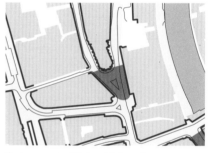

Gateway to Walcot Street.

Creation of new destination space including installation of public art.

Reconfiguration of traffic movements through the area to reduce area used by vehicular traffic and to enhance the pedestrian experience.

Intimate spaces

1 Corn Market Square

Creation of a new space as setting for the refurbished Corn Market building. This space would provide a gateway space to Walcot Street and enable pedestrian access to the River Corridor and a potential new footbridge link to Henrietta Park. The space would also be enclosed by new building frontage resulting from the redevelopment of the cattle market site. This space has the potential to accommodate activity linked to the Walcot Street area including specialist markets, street performance, and outdoor café and seating.

2 Broad Street Place

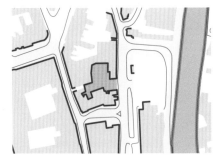

Repaving and landscaping of this hidden space on the route from Broad Street to Walcot Street. Proposals will complement the planned installation of a William Pye water sculpture.

3 Rear of the Guildhall

This intimate space is on an alternative route linking Orange Grove to Grand Parade. There are opportunities for a repaving of this area and extension or improved connections into the Covered Market and the opening up of routes via the little known East Gate to The River Corridor, the vaults underneath Grand Parade and Bridge Street, and onto Parade Gardens.

4 Abbey Green

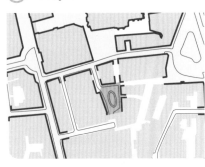

Enhanced maintenance and management of an area with an existing high quality public realm.

Introduce traffic measures to exclude non-essential vehicles using this space.

5 Burial Ground

Re-landscaping to enhance spatial qualities and to improve physical linkages to adjoining Arts Centre.

Introduction of bespoke street furniture.

6 Green Park Station Forecourt

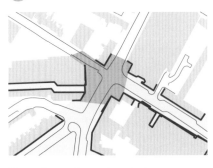

Repaving using natural stone.

Introduce natural stone to pedestrian crossings to enhance gateway to Bath Western Riverside regeneration area.

Parks, gardens and recreational spaces

① Hedgemead Park

Provision of improved pedestrian access including enhanced gateways, facilities and landscape design measures to improve views into and out of the park. This park is currently under-utilised and largely unknown to visitors. It enables pedestrian connections to Camden Crescent where panoramic views of the city can be enjoyed.

② Walcot Gate Park

Re-landscaping of under-utilised playing field accessed off Walcot Gate. To include provision of pedestrian link from River Corridor walkway to Walcot Street retail spine. Although set on a slope, this space, with skilful landscape design and the provision of facilities, could provide a setting for passive recreation and small scale events.

③ Henrietta Park

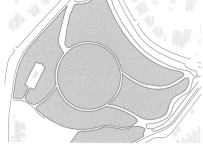

Enhancement of park to reflect destination status in parallel with improved pedestrian and cycle connections. Currently this valuable green space is an under-utilised asset but has the potential to act as a venue for a wide range of activity including organised events. It's proximity to Great Pulteney Street, the Holburne Museum and Sydney Gardens needs to be exploited more effectively.

④ Sydney Gardens

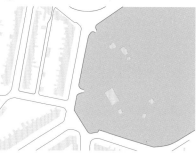

Sydney Gardens, a Grade 2 Listed 18th century pleasure garden that was created as part of an overall development plan for the Pulteney Estate on land East of the River Avon. Linked to the city centre by the newly constructed Pulteney Bridge and Great Pulteney Street, Sydney Gardens became a social hub of city life. It incorporated a range of attractions including a grotto and swings and was animated by a programme of entertainment including musical performances and fireworks. These 'Vauxhall' style gardens became a favoured place for the fashionable people of Bath to promenade and play. The Bath Guide even claimed that 'this garden, for beauty of situation and variety of elegant scenes cannot be surpassed by any pleasure ground in the Kingdom'.

In view of the recent development scheme to extend the Holburne Museum, there is a tremendous opportunity for this to complement a revival of Sydney Gardens as a key city destination. A Heritage Lottery Fund bid for the Gardens is currently under development.

The combination of a remodelled Holburne Museum and a refreshed Sydney Gardens will create a new city attraction and opportunities to encourage a 21st century revival of the pleasure garden concept. The Public Realm and Movement Strategy recognises the importance of connectivity between the city centre and Sydney Gardens and recommends improvements to Grand Parade, Pulteney Bridge and Great Pulteney Street.

⑤ Recreation Ground

Improved pedestrian connections and access from The River Corridor walkway, new foot bridge crossing and connections to Laura Place will help to tackle pedestrian congestion related to major sporting events, and support new initiatives to broaden the activities hosted at these venues.

Parks, gardens and recreational spaces

⑥ Parade Gardens

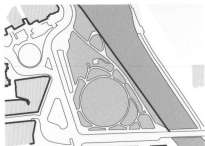

Proposal to work with all owners of the site to explore the following options:

Remodelling of the gardens to create a 21st century pleasure garden. Improvements could include open pedestrian access from Terrace Walk, Orange Grove and Grand Parade. Re-landscaping to create improved relationship with the river and River Corridor walkway, including a potential new footbridge crossing to the Recreation Ground and East bank River Corridor walkway; temporary and permanent works of public art and craft; potential to provide a significant venue for outdoor performances and events of a city scale.

New pedestrian link with Terrace Walk/York Street.

Contemporary and sustainable re-landscaping of the gardens to include measures to facilitate and accommodate events/performances; repair and stabilisation of Western perimeter boundary elevated roadway; coordinated lighting scheme; integration of major water feature.

New River Corridor parade to link with North River Corridor path.

Link to emerging ideas to redevelop the undercroft of the former Empire Hotel, to enhance the Guidhall complex and to reveal medieval remains under bridge Street and Slippery Lane.

Investigate potential of lighting North Parade Bridge, reinstating the missing lamp, and re-opening access to Parade Gardens from North Parade.

⑦ Green Park

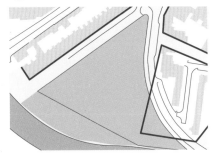

Enhancement of this major green space to improve its role as a location for passive recreation; improved pedestrian and cycle links to The River Corridor walkway. Enhancement proposals should form part of an integrated urban design framework for the 'North Quays' area.

⑧ Norfolk Crescent

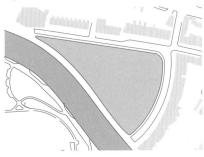

Provision of improved pedestrian access including linkages to The River Corridor and landscape design measures to improve views into and out of the park.

⑨ Royal Victoria Park

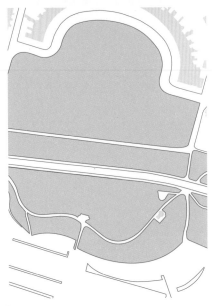

This is the city's largest park, hosting a vast array of both formal and informal activities, and offering different spaces for different uses. It has recently benefited from significant investment from the Heritage Lottery Fund. However, there are further opportunities to enhance the user experience of the park through the extension of the wayfinding system and through improvements in the physical connections to it, for example through the widening of the footway between Queen Square and entrance to Royal Victoria Park and displacement of car parking, and restoring Grand Walk to its former glory.

Footnote

It is noted that ambitions for certain parks and green spaces may be limited by covenants or other legal restrictions and therefore all proposals are subject to further investigation.

Integrating regeneration areas into the spatial structure of the city

Major new development sites have been identified across the city centre in recent years at the Cattlemarket/Hilton Hotel site, Guildhall and environs, Manvers Street, Bath Quays (North and South of the river), the area West of Kingsmead Square, Green Park House and Kingsmead House and at Bath Western Riverside. In many of these areas, the spatial structure is disconnected from the historic core of the city centre. These areas need to be stitched back into the fabric of the city, with their streets and spaces designed to reflect the city's core design values. There is a real risk that if these regeneration areas are not treated as part of or as an extension to the wider city centre, that they will become self-contained quarters, each with its own approach to urban and streetscape design. This will only undermine the essence of Bath as a total composition, adding further layers of confusion.

It is recommended, therefore, that the network of streets and spaces within these new development areas should be inspired by and respond to the existing pattern and rhythm of streets and spaces within the city centre, taking account of distinctive Bath features such as the relationship of building entrances and active edges and the scale, form and massing of buildings.

As an example, the layout of streets and spaces in the Avon Street/Bath Quays area should be designed to connect to surrounding areas, helping to ensure that the new development is properly integrated with the historic heart of the city, the new SouthGate, The River Corridor and the Green Park area. The masterplanning of proposals for new development areas within or adjacent to the centre must therefore be conceived and designed with the objective to create strong physical and visual connections with surrounding parts of the centre, responding and contributing to the overall Public Realm and Movement Plan. With this approach, Bath's public realm represents the glue to bind together new and historic parts of the city, helping to create one enlarged, coherent and connected centre.

In support of this approach, all sites that fall within the proposed boundary of the expanded city centre, should utilise the same natural stone street surfaces, wayfinding and transport products and new street furniture specified for the city centre, again reinforcing the sense of a larger, more unified centre.

Integrating the river into the spatial structure of the city

The majority of Bath's key future regeneration sites, including The Podium, the Guildhall, the Recreation Ground, Manvers Street, Bath Quays and Bath Western Riverside, all share a direct relationship with the river. New flood-plain regulations and policies often restrict the development potential of these sites and add cost and complexity to proposals. However, this should not deter Bath from learning from the world's best examples of riverside regeneration and using new development to unlock the enormous potential of its river and canal for the wider benefit and wellbeing of the city and its people.

In addition to the potential of future regeneration sites, there are many other opportunities for revealing and enjoying the river as a key element of Bath's public realm:

INTEGRATING THE RIVER INTO THE SPATIAL STRUCTURE OF THE CITY
Delivery of proposed new pedestrian bridges crossing the river at key nodal points connecting to the network of streets and spaces illustrated in the Public Realm and Movement Plan – through new development schemes.
Creation of a green corridor along the river forming a series of linked River Corridor spaces and providing a variety of active and peaceful areas along the river edge.
Support the creation of river-related businesses, and creating opportunities for more active uses associated with it, eg. voids underneath Grand Parade. Ensure that any future detailed proposals for the area take account of the need to submit a supporting Flood Risk Assessment.
Enhancing walking and cycling circuits along the River Corridor and connecting to different parts of the city.
Improving the quality of connections between the Kennet and Avon Canal and the River Avon.
Implementation of the Walcot River Corridor Path.
Introduction of river-based leisure or public transport.
More water-based events from the fun (raft races) to the competitive (national sporting events).
Creation of a Festival of Water and Wellbeing that combines the use of the river, the Thermae Spa and the Roman Baths.
Reinforcing the ecological role of the river as a green corridor, and a sanctuary for wildlife, whilst balancing the aspiration to improve access for the public.
Consideration of future potential for river swimming, lidos and urban beaches in Bath, which have recently experienced a revival in a number of European cities.

Proposed projects – riverscape

The re-integration of the riverscape into the spatial structure of the city centre and wider area will help to reinvigorate the role of the river and adjoining buildings and spaces in the city's public life. The proposed projects, to be delivered via future development schemes, will help to improve access to the riverscape and pedestrian movement along its entire length through the phased improvement of existing paths and the introduction of new sections to create a continuous River Corridor walkway. Access and linkages will further be improved and a series of walking circuits promoted by the introduction of up to six new river crossings, primarily for pedestrians and cyclists and improved connections and vertical access to existing bridges. Any new bridge crossings are subject to the Environment Agency's Flood Defence Consent process. There will be a need to objectively balance this against any possible increase in flood risk posed by any new crossing and/or any restriction to navigation, specifically on the reach downstream of Pulteney Weir.

The proposed sitings for new pedestrian bridges are not fixed at this stage. The case for any additional crossing at Norfolk Crescent would need to be demonstrated, including consideration of the impact on local residents (Local Plan policy D2).

Proposed projects –
riverscape

1 River Corridor North
2 River Corridor Central
3 River Corridor South
4 The Quays
5 River Corridor West

■ Destination spaces
▦ River Corridor walkway
--→ Improved linkages
— Proposed new/
improved bridges

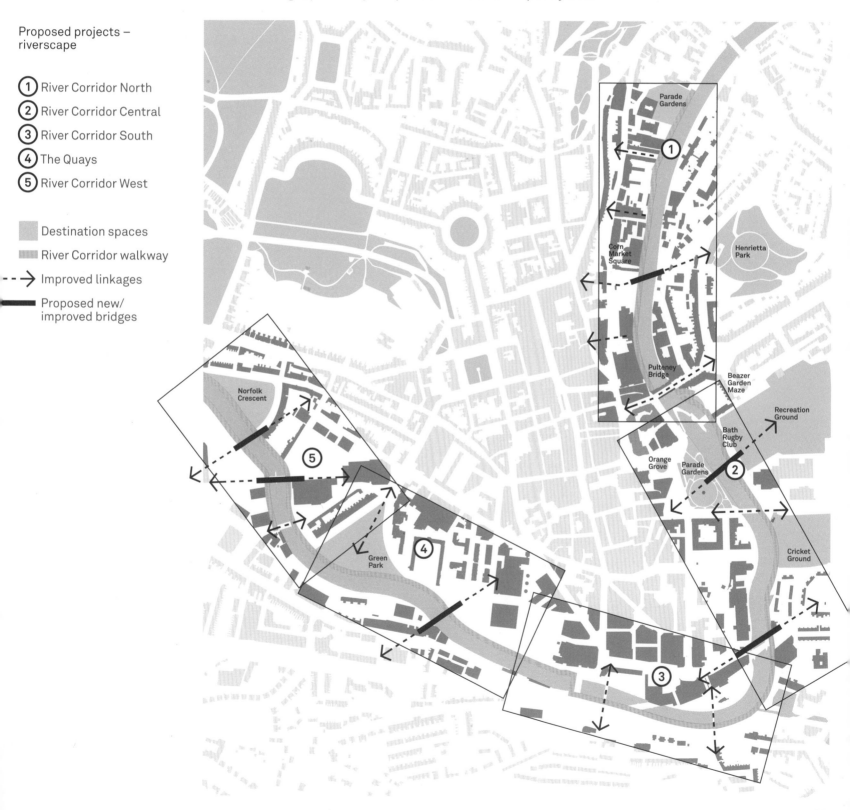

Riverscape

① River Corridor North

River Corridor Walkway including boardwalk section linking Pulteney Bridge, via Podium, Cattlemarket redevelopment, new public space at the Cornmarket up to renewed public park at Walcot Gate Park.

Enhanced pedestrian connections from the walkway to Walcot Street will form part of a wider supporting package of improvements helping to boost footfall in the Walcot Street area by the creation of appealing walking circuits.

② River Corridor Central

Parade Gardens River Corridor Promenade to be complemented by an enhanced promenading walkway on the East bank to include street furniture and lighting and seating areas.

Rationalisation and enhancement of mooring/landing stage, landscaped space and Beazer Garden adjacent to river sluice gate.

Potential removal or modification of sluice gate mechanism, subject to consultation with Environment Agency.

Improvements to pedestrian access from Argyle Street and North Parade Bridge.

③ River Corridor South

Potential new pedestrian bridge cantilevered from North face of railway bridge linking to Railway Station/Manvers Street/ SouthGate area.

General upgrading improvements to existing River Corridor path including removal/cutting back of overgrown areas to reveal views and improve community safety, kiosk structures with seating areas and lighting.

New River Corridor parade to link with North River Corridor path.

New pedestrian bridge link to East bank River Corridor promenade and Recreation Ground.

Potential lighting scheme to associated Brunel structures.

④ The Quays

Improved River Corridor promenade/linear River Corridor park connecting to Green Park and Broad Quay/Dorchester Street.

Enhancements to Green Park.

New pedestrian footbridge link to South Quays and residential areas beyond.

⑤ River Corridor West

General upgrading improvements to existing River Corridor North bank path including removal/ cutting back of overgrown areas to reveal views and improve community safety, kiosk structures with seating areas and lighting.

New River Corridor path created via Bath Western Riverside regeneration project.

Composite map of streets and space to be improved

Streets

Arrival and departure spaces

Destination squares and spaces

Intimate spaces

Parks, gardens and recreational spaces

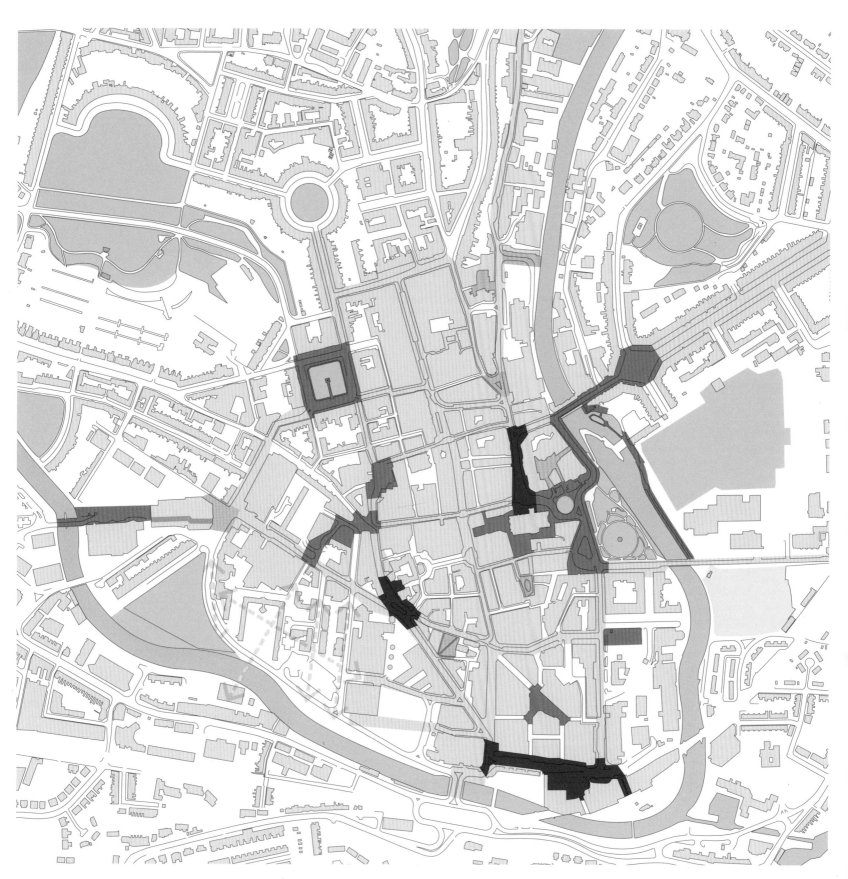

3: A CITY REVEALED THROUGH A NEW CITY INFORMATION SYSTEM

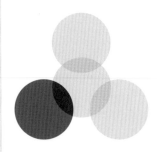

A new city information system will be at the heart of Bath's regeneration over the coming decade connecting destinations, spaces and streets and improving legibility for people who work in, visit and enjoy the city.

Introduction – key issues

Information plays an essential role in ensuring that residents and visitors – whether in the city on business, for learning or for leisure – make the most of their time and have an enjoyable experience of Bath. A city information system not only helps people to understand, access and enjoy the city, it also plays a vital role in attracting new visitors and ensuring the journey to and from the city is as easy and stress-free as possible. Information is the means by which people can understand and interact with the physical place.

The requirement for a world-class information system for Bath is unquestionable. There are three essential factors that make a compelling case for putting a coherent, high quality information system at the heart of the city's future revitalisation. These factors have emerged through preliminary research and observation. It will be essential to undertake testing and market research to evaluate and evolve the proposed strategy, basing it firmly on an evidence base. This research could include visitor profiling, pedestrian modelling and demand forecasting for products and services. The quantitative and qualitative results will form a solid base for developing projects.

Meeting user needs. This is an information-rich age. It has never been easier to access information and the means by which people can search, access and interact with information has never been more sophisticated. Increasingly, we demand and expect information that is tailored to our interests and needs and often we research and want to experience a city even before we have decided to visit.

Painting a picture of Bath. Many visitors struggle to find and experience the Bath they expected. The area visitors explore is often limited by their 'mental map' of the city, leaving them feeling disorientated when straying far from the key retail spines. There is evidence of "I've done the Roman Baths, what else is there?" syndrome, indicating a gap in how the city, its destinations and spaces are revealed and understood.

Communicating the city. The quality and design values underpinning existing information do not represent or interpret the values and attributes of Bath as a city. Information is not consistent or designed as a coherent system, leading to a lack of understanding of the city as a whole. As the physical city undergoes a transformation and creates a high quality, pedestrian-friendly environment, information will play a key role in communicating these values to visitors before they arrive and during their stay; and to residents and workers as part of their everyday life.

Objectives

The objectives in developing any information system should centre on the quality, relevance, accessibility and level of connectivity with other information systems.

For Bath, the demands on the information system are high. The range of activities and needs of different people in the city are broad. The future vision and development proposals for the city present a challenge which does not prohibit the development of a system itself, but does increase the pressure for it to function, be able to grow and be sustained. The following objectives must be met to ensure this aspiration is met.

_Information must meet the needs of users.
_Products and services must be designed to be user-friendly, intuitive and accessible to all.

_The system must be future-proofed, be easy to manage and maintain.
_Products should make the best and most relevant use of technologies.
_The system should share a single identity that speaks of the values of the city.
_The visual design and content must celebrate and promote the city – its history, heritage and culture.

The information system must recognise the needs and limitations of all users, of all ages and ability. The development of the system will be guided by best practice and be compliant with the Disability Discrimination Act (DDA).

user needs
Five user scenarios provide a snapshot of information needs which help identify the attributes required of a successful information system for Bath

	Time rich				Time poor
Who are they?	Resident	Weekend visitor – heritage trip	Family visit	Day visitor – shopper	Business visitor
What do they want to do?	Regular trips – might want to explore further.	Discover historic Bath, relax.	Relax and enjoy the city.	Shop 'til they drop.	Get to a meeting on time.
What do they need?	Real-time transport information. What's on, news, events.	Itineraries, ideas. Interpretation of the city's features. Places to relax.	Activity ideas for all age groups. Best spaces to take a break. Stress-free travel in and out of the centre.	Shopping guide. Easy/quick journey in and out of the city.	Fast, efficient transport. 'Mental map' and simple routes. Online information.
Objectives of the information system	Immediate access to up-to-date travel information. Event related information. Extend 'mental map' of the city.	Provide guides, slow-read mapping and information. Illustrate the whole city and the connections between things.	Provide tailored travel solutions. Clear indication of distances and access. Show facilities such as toilets, play areas etc.	Provide detailed mapping to show shopping areas. Interactive tools to plan visit. Simple travel plan from home to Bath and back.	Provide up-to-date travel information. Simple city centre print map.
Aims/benefits	Improve day-to-day experience, extend activity, encourage walking and less car use.	Ensure basic navigation of the city is easy. Create an excellent first impression.	Ensure a stress-free visit, real benefits of a people-friendly city. Encourage a longer stay or return visit.	Extend usual 'mental map' of the city. Combine information to encourage longer stay for other activities.	Help them make the best choices. Create a good impression, encourage longer stay or repeat visit with friends or family.

The strategy: all modes; whole journey; all media channels

Central to the concept for an information system for Bath is the need to deliver a seamless, connected system of products that cross delivery channels and modes of travel. The concept is illustrated on the following pages by an information journey – starting at the point of researching at home through to arriving in and moving around the city.

Using best practice examples from other cities, it shows how a holistic approach to information provision is a necessary component in making Bath a world class city in which to live, work, visit and play for all types of users.

To ensure users can access what they need in a format and at the location they need it, the system must respond and be tailored to a set of requirements that make up any journey. The concept is to ensure that each stage of the journey is supported by the relevant information and tools whether it is pre-arrival, en route to the city, on arrival, while you are travelling around, or at a destination.

An information system for Bath will balance the need to provide a highly detailed view of the city to encourage exploration and deliver the level of information required, with a structured and hierarchical network of travel routes that works seamlessly to connect the city's destinations, areas and spaces. The concept will direct the development of three principle levels of delivery: orientation, navigation and exploring.

Through careful planning the aim will be to minimise the number of products required, so as to reduce clutter within the city's streets and spaces.

AN INFORMATION SYSTEM FOR BATH

A multi-modal wayfinding and information system. Not just for pedestrian movement, but all vehicular modes including private car, cycling and public transport: Bath Rapid Transit and Showcase Bus Routes.

A multi-channel wayfinding and information system. Not just signs, but wayfinding and information services delivered through print, web and other digital and mobile media.

A system of products and services that are planned and designed to connect, not just the walking part, but all stages of the journey.

A system unique to Bath

An information system for Bath will be designed, developed and delivered in a way that will reflect, build and support the city's underlying DNA, physical attributes and design values. A highly structured, hierarchical system will ensure that the minimum amount of physical products are put into the streets and spaces of the city. With careful information planning and product design, the system should limit the amount of street clutter – physical objects whose detrimental effect on the streetscape and movement within it outweighs any benefits of the information it carries.

There are a number of ways in which the design of the city information system will ensure that values such as lightness of touch are upheld.

Soft over hard products. Particular attention will be given to print and digital products and people services so that street signs are less depended on and also provide solutions that are more flexible and cost effective to maintain.

Just where it's needed. Information products will be carefully located to maximise use and be most effective in providing different information types.

Less is more. Graphic design and planning of information will ensure that the maximum amount is communicated with the most efficient use of space. Visual design will be informed by a set of values that reflect the city around it – symmetry, proportion, balance – to ensure the displays can sit comfortably in the surrounding composition.

Form. Products themselves will be bespoke to the information they need to carry and be constructed from materials informed by the design values of the city and that – together with other street furniture – create a composition.

The following pages illustrate the potential scope of the information journey. All the images in this section are selected from best practice to demonstrate, by example, the potential range of information products and services that will form Bath's City Information System (CIS).

best practice
This indicative journey has been illustrated with examples of information products and services developed in other major UK cities. Many of these projects, now considered best practice, illustrate the application of high-quality information planning and graphic identity within information systems.

 How do I get to Bath by car?
Can I download a carpark map?

 What shops are available?
Can I create an itinerary?
How do I get to the park & ride?

08.00am

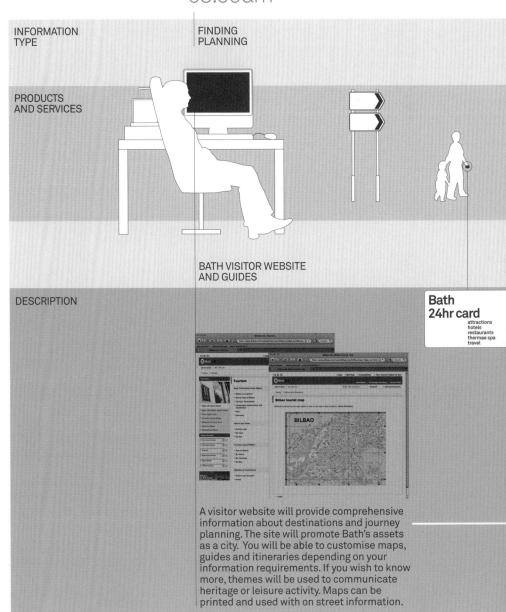

INFORMATION TYPE	FINDING PLANNING
PRODUCTS AND SERVICES	

BATH VISITOR WEBSITE AND GUIDES

DESCRIPTION

Bath 24hr card
attractions
hotels
restaurants
thermae spa
travel

A visitor website will provide comprehensive information about destinations and journey planning. The site will promote Bath's assets as a city. You will be able to customise maps, guides and itineraries depending on your information requirements. If you wish to know more, themes will be used to communicate heritage or leisure activity. Maps can be printed and used with on street information.

whole journey

The user experience will be dramatically enhanced by taking a whole journey, coordinated approach to services and products. The user, whether they be a visitor or resident, will gain a greater understanding of the city and have a more enjoyable experience when provided with consistent, high quality information at all stages of the journey.

total composition

Presenting the city centre as a total composition reinforces the sense of unity and continuity through streets and spaces. Ensuring the complete landscape is always with you as you move around the city centre, reinforces a mental map – connecting destinations and aiding orientation.

How big is the city centre?
What are the must do or must sees?
Where are the destinations?
Where are the transport interchanges?
What's essential information?
How can we find out more?

Where are the destinations?
Where are transport interchanges?
What are the must do or must sees?
What's essential information?
How can we find out more?

── 10.00am ──

── 11.00am ──

ORIENTATION

NAVIGATION

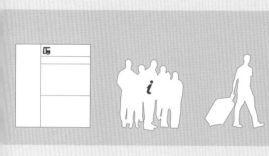
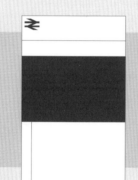

WELCOME POINT

WALK MAPS

ase maps
set of master base maps ill be drawn from which dividual map products can e cut and rotated for use.

Consistency of information
Map bases, visual styling and nomenclature will be introduced to those who choose to pre-plan, they will be consistent and compatible with the user experience within the city centre.

Companions
Information products and services designed as one system work together to aid user wayfinding.

On arrival, welcome information points will display the whole composition of the city centre, highlighting strategic transport connections and principal pedestrian routes connecting the city's primary destinations, its architectural set-pieces and public spaces. An index will help you to locate streets and destinations easily.

Free printed maps will be available across the city in hotels, destinations, restaurants, businesses and Tourist Information Centres. Easy to carry with you they will present the whole composition of the city whilst highlighting key areas, destinations and services.

Where are the shopping highlights?
Where are the transport interchanges?

 Where are we?
Where are the Roman Baths?
What's on the way there?

 Where am I?
Where are the shopping areas?

11.30am ─────────────────────── ## 12.00am ───────────────────

LEARNING
EXPLORING

RE-ORIENTATION
DIRECTING

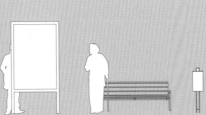
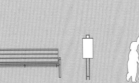

THEMED MAPS

INFORMATION SYSTEM

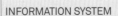

Landmarks
Illustrated landmark
buildings – used across
mapping products – will
highlight the city's primary
sights and provide useful
points of orientation.

Always with you
An overview map will be
located at every information
point and is rotated to match
the area map and your
viewpoint – helping you
orientate yourself within
the wider area.

Themed maps and guides will be available
in multiple languages and versions, tailored
to your interests. Guides will be available
across the city in hotels, destinations,
restaurants, businesses and Tourist
Information Centres. Easy to carry with
you they will uncover information relevant
to your chosen theme or themes.

Located at key points of decision
making, panels will provide
detailed area mapping to help you
find your destination and show
you the way to get there. A simple
prospect of the city centre will
build a mental map of the city and
assure you of where you are in
relation to the wider area and
principal transport interchanges.

walkable city

Putting the pedestrian first. Providing tailored views of the city: a detailed plan to a scale to suit your speed with crossings, steps and entrances marked. Creating a hierarchy of information that promotes walking; showing the places to promenade, areas to stroll, the quick routes, the short cuts, the interesting lanes and alleys, somewhere to relax and take in the view.

single identity

A single integrated information system will be built that presents a consistent visual identity of graphic and information design elements and product designs that develop the city's identity and that are inspired by the city itself.

The golden section, proportions that are found throughout the city will provide a visual structure for information levels.

How can we get around the city?
Where can we get to?
Where are the stops and interchanges?

Can I get across town quickly?
When and how frequent are the services?

— 1.00pm

JOURNEY PLANNING

— 2.00pm

ON ROUTE
ON BOARD

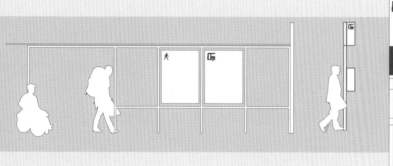

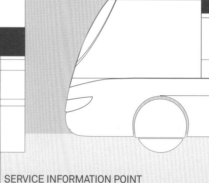

Bath Rapid Transit   Route 1

TRAVEL INFORMATION POINT
AND SHELTER

SERVICE INFORMATION POINT

ON BOARD INFORMATION

Distance indicator
A walk distance will always be displayed clearly to show you the size of the area or city as a whole. This allows you to plan your journey more accurately and promotes Bath as a walkable city.

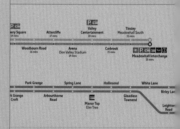

Consistent language and information planning ensure that bus information is seamless with pedestrian information, encouraging use of public transport and making the interchange between modes and the onward journey on foot as easy as possible.

A local area map, together with a simple prospect of the city centre will help you to re-orientate yourself and locate nearby services when alighting from a bus service.

Onward journey information
Integrated transport information enables you to switch between modes of transport with ease, allowing you to explore the city and plan your onward journey.

A simple diagrammatic map will remain with you so that you can understand your route and plan your onward journey.

networked

The system will be designed to work at the level of the complete city centre as well as linking inwardly and outwardly to neighbouring communities, city wide destinations and the region.

intuitive

Products and services will be designed to comply with legibility guidelines and allow for instant interpretation. Through the use of 'heads-up' mapping – orientated to match the view in front of the user – and 'walk distance' measurements, all information will be integrated and easily understood.

Where are we?
What can we see?
What's significant?

Where are we?
What's significant about this place?

Where am I?
Where are the shops I want?
How far?

3.30pm

4.30pm

ENJOYING
UNDERSTANDING

GUIDING
FINDING

ALFRED STREET

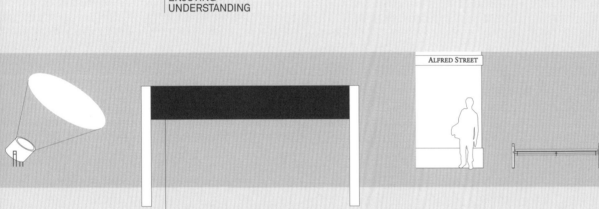

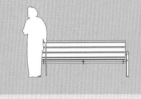

INTERPRETATION
VISTA POINT

DIRECTORY PANEL

A vista point displays a complete landscape elevation of a vista or complete prospect of a city view. Relevant themed information will be available for those who wish to enjoy and learn more about the city.

Themed information
Specific information is disclosed based on theme adding context and interest to the streets and spaces. A directory for finding is available when in an area of shopping, activity or major significance.

Interpretation & public art
Interpretive information will play an important role in representing and understanding the historical city of Bath. Subtle features work alongside map-based information to enhance user experience.

Located at key points of interest or activity providing detailed information about the immediate area. A simple prospect of the city centre will be accompanied by a directory of stores in a shopping area and an explanation of significant places or spaces within a place of interest.

future proofed
The information system will be
developed in a way to ensure it
can be kept up to date, managed
and maintained by the project
partners within the structure of
the proposed Bath Pattern Book.

When is the next train home?
Where is good to eat?

─── 5.00pm ───

FINDING
JOURNEY PLANNING

HAND HELD INFORMATION SERVICES

Mobile technology
A multi-channel information
system allows you to make
the most of all technology
available. This approach allows
for maximum compatibility
between on street and digital
information provision.

Directories
Helping you to locate
attractions and
destinations quickly and
easily. Information may
be listed alphabetically
with a map reference.

Hand held mobile devices and
mobile applications can
be utilised to complement your
journey within the city. You will
be able to use hand held
technology to plan your onward
journey or use GPS technology
for navigation. Devices may also
be used to receive on street
interpretive information,
triggered by a area of interest.

Building on the city's visual legacy

The extensive body of work showing prospects of the city by figures such as Samuel and Nathanial Buck and illustrations of spaces such as Queen Square by Thomas Malton the Younger has provided the city of Bath with a rich and visually powerful legacy of mapping and illustration.

By learning and being informed by this source of historic design work, the city can benefit not only in terms of ensuring the quality and artistry of design and illustration is upheld, but also through ensuring that the cartographic and design approach is grounded in something very personal and unique to the city.

The diagram below illustrates how the three views of illustrating the city historically – prospect, plan and elevation – can be exploited to meet the needs of users at different points in their journey. This tailoring of the way the city is portrayed builds on the legacy of city mapping and – by implementing design principles, such as heads-up mapping and appropriate scale – the system will provide the user with the relevant tools to suit their wayfinding needs.

Creating the design resources for the city

Cartography and mapping will become an important tool for delivering projects and will form a large part of a set of a resources that will be created for the city. Typography, pictograms, colour references, copy, materials and techniques will all be developed to enable the roll out of city information projects. These resources will be collated and managed as part of the proposed Bath Pattern Book.

right
A New and Correct Plan of the City of Bath – detail 1817

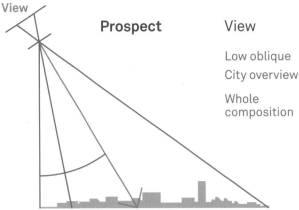

Prospect	View	Orientation
	Low oblique	Arrival planning
	City overview	Mental map
	Whole composition	Transport network mapping

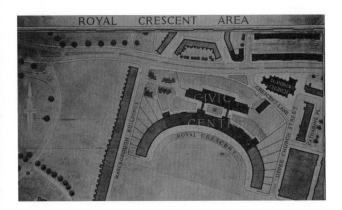
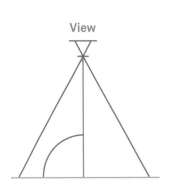

Plan	View	Navigation
	Aerial	Finding
		Direction

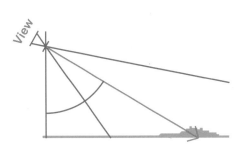

Elevation	View	Exploring
	Panoramic	Interpretation
	Vista	Guide/finding

A NEW
AND CORRECT PLAN
of the
CITY OF BATH
from a recent Survey

REFERENCES

1	Abbey Church	13	Pump Room
2	St Michaels Church	14	Kings and Queen's Bath
3	St James Church	15	Cross Bath
4	Walcot Church	16	Hot Bath
5	New or Christs Church	17	Hot Bath Pump Room
6	St Johns Chapel	18	Kingston Bath
7	King Street Chapel	19	General Hospital
8	Moravian Chapel	20	City Dispensary
9	Roman Catholic Chapel	21	Casualty Hospital
10	Quakers Meeting	22	Theatre
11	Unitarian Meeting		The Names of the other Public Buildings
12	Blue Coat Charity School		are in their respective Places

95

Proposed key projects

Bath visitor web site

Develop and extend the existing Visit Bath website that manages a visitors 'first point of touch' experience of Bath and/or create a new website to provide information content that is tailored to user requirements and an enhanced experience in terms of guiding, journey planning, attraction and destination finding. The website will:

Introduce Bath's unique visual identity to the visitor at the start of their journey experience – planning their journey on the world wide web.

Provide a geographic overview of the city to reveal Bath's unique setting, walkable scale and main visitor attractions.

Provide visitor itinerary planning tools – to reveal Bath's wider city offer and encourage longer stays.

Interactive mapping suite to create your own unique themed maps and guides of the city.

Introduce Bath's exemplary pedestrian environment, car free central area and encourage visitors to use public transport and Park & Ride to travel to and around the city.

Walk map

Develop a free printed visitor map for pedestrians which can be distributed through main points of arrival, transport interchanges, tourist information centres, attractions, destinations, accommodation providers, universities and other third parties. Content to include:

Visitor information.

Attractions and destinations.

Interpretation.

Pedestrian routes.

Transport connections.

Content indices.

Themed maps/guides

Develop a range of themed maps and guides to connect attractions, destinations and points of interest.

To be provided in multilingual versions.

Themes could include: heritage and culture, shopping, Bath after 5pm, city centre walks and parks and gardens.

Available in printed format from main points of arrival, transport interchanges, tourist information centres, attractions, destinations, accommodation providers and other third parties.

Digital information services

Develop a digital information strategy for the provision of information services to static digital information points and dynamic hand held mobile devices.

Develop contextualised mapping information for interactive online and on-street digital use.

Review and audit technology to adopt a future proof approach to providing, managing and maintaining visitor information that can be accessed by hand held mobile technology.

Arrival points

Develop information signs at key points of arrival including Bath Spa station, Park and Ride sites, bus station, coach parks, primary car parks and Bristol International Airport to provide welcoming visitor information and point of orientation for navigation and onward journey planning. Information to include:

Welcome to Bath, World Heritage Site.

An overview or prospect map to allow users to view the whole composition of the city. Users will be able to understand its distance, structure and physical relationship of destinations. In a simplified form, this composition will be a consistent element that remains with you as you move around the city.

Instructions on how to get around the city.

Onward journey planning information.

Primary visitor information including primary attractions and destinations and interpretation, pedestrian routes and transport connections.

Content indices.

Pedestrian signs

Develop pedestrian information signs to be located at key decision making points in the city centre. Information will include:

A street level of mapping, in a heads up format, that will enable people to navigate their next step through the city and find nearest destinations or facilities.

A map of the extended city centre for orientation within the wider context of the city.

Primary visitor information including primary attractions and destinations and interpretation, pedestrian routes and transport connections.

Content indices.

Shopping directories

Develop a range of information directories to provide visitors with detailed information about their immediate area.

Shopping directories to allow shoppers to find specific destinations quickly or to identify the full extent of retail options available.

Food and drink directories.

Information directories at key destinations and attractions.

Interpretation points

Develop a range of interpretation products such as historical plaques, interpretation signs, city vista displays and public art interpretation, to provide information about Bath to enhance a visitors experience through engaging, revealing, understanding, discovering and learning. Interpretation products will include:

Detailed guides, indexes or interpretation will be provided annotating an elevation of the view. Information will help users explore the area in greater detail.

Historical interpretation.

Reveal further points of interest in Bath.

Restore incised lettering of street names.

Links to further information.

The plan that follows illustrates how, through research of pedestrian flow counts in the city centre, the routes and spaces of Bath can be assessed to form a pedestrian route hierarchy. This process relies on close assessment of current and future development sites in the city to ensure these are connected into the network. The primary pedestrian routes and secondary connecting routes link arrival points and destinations in the city, guiding the location and orientation of the four basic types of information products.

The indicative location of products form a core network which will, in time, be extended into new development areas such as Bath Quays.

Bath city centre
Pedestrian Footfall
Counts, May 2006

left
60 city centre count
points that cover the
retail area.

right
Density of
pedestrian flow.

Red =
High pedestrian flow
>40,000

Orange =
Medium pedestrian flow
20,000 to 40,000

Yellow =
Low pedestrian flow
< 20,000

All figures are based on
average weekly footfall.

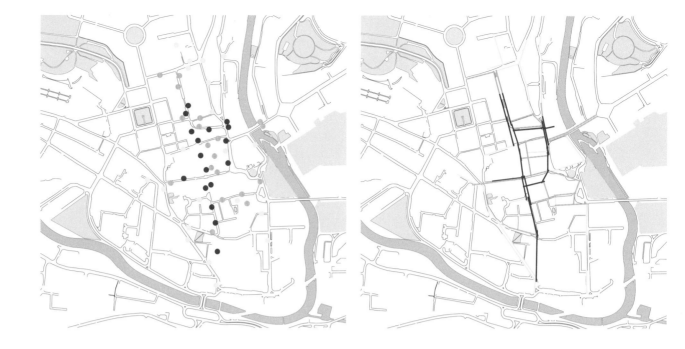

Proposed pedestrian
route hierarchy

▬ Primary routes

▬ Secondary routes

▬ Tertiary routes

● Arrival points

● Pedestrian signs

○ Directories

○ Interpretation
points

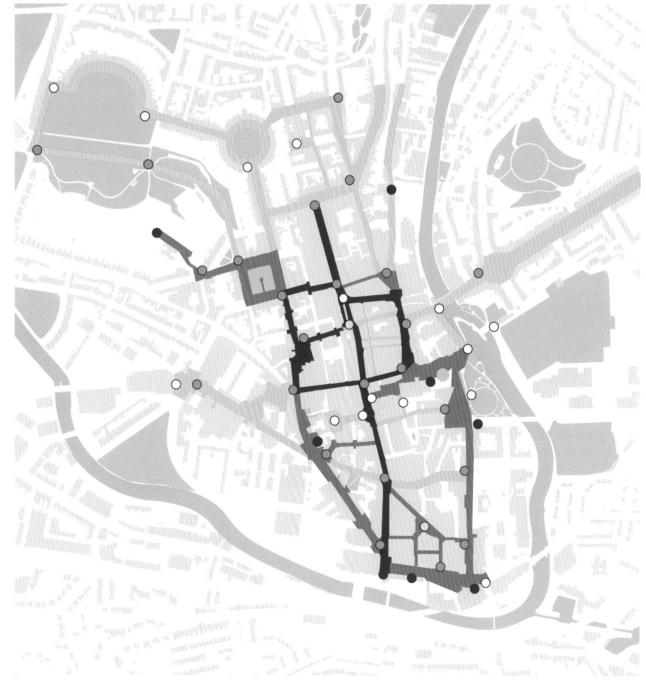

4: A CANVAS FOR PUBLIC LIFE

A city reanimated

The big idea to rebalance and refashion Bath's public realm and movement systems in order to create a canvas for public life and wellbeing is given form and direction in the Public Realm and Movement Plan. It is given further depth and structure through the understanding and integration of the layers of the Composing Elements and its character and design quality will be shaped and controlled through the Design Elements within the emerging Bath Pattern Book.

However, in addition to the availability of funding and investment, the realisation, delivery and success of the Canvas for Public Life ultimately depends on strong creative leadership, coordinated and effective management and maintenance and, not least, on the development of a bold, imaginative and exciting programme of cultural and community animation to reinvigorate the vibrancy, image and appeal of Bath as a city.

Once again, this suggests a return to the spirit of the 18th century when elements such as outstanding design, cutting edge culture and pleasure, health and wellbeing and entrepreneurial activity were creatively balanced and orchestrated in order to re-imagine and re-position Bath as one of Europe's finest cities. Approaching the art of city-making in Bath from a 21st century perspective requires similar levels of ambition, creativity and persistence. It also demands the ability to think differently, in a more rounded way, in order to see the connections between things.

An orchestra without a conductor – overcoming fragmented thinking

In order to understand and harness the future potential of the city, an overarching sense of Bath city centre as a place is required, where seemingly disparate or fragmented interests, services and agendas, ways of thinking, knowledge and skill bases can be aligned and melded into a whole, like the composition of a great piece of music.

The responsibility for and the creative direction of this task – the question of who should be the conductor of the orchestra – demands active consideration and resolution. With regard to the management of the city centre, it is encouraging that Future Bath Plus has recently been established. This public and private sector entity has brought together the management of the city centre (including the appointment of a City Centre Manager) with that of Bath Tourism Plus and with the involvement of the cultural sector. Hopefully this signals the beginning of a more integrated and coherent future for the city centre. It is hoped that the Public Realm and Movement Strategy will guide and inform the agenda and work plan for Future Bath Plus. It is also encouraging that the Council has been restructured to bring most of the relevant services involved in the management of the public realm into one area. A number of the proposals contained within the Public Realm and Movement Strategy offer a real opportunity for the Council to pioneer new management practices in a project context.

The renaissance of Bath's public realm

The proposed delivery of the Public Realm and Movement Strategy in the centre of Bath over the next 10 to 20 years unlocks huge opportunities for the city. Handled with imagination and flair and with a sense of Bath's distinctiveness, originality and authenticity, this could result in a renaissance in urban living, cultural expression, economic success, environmental sustainability and health and wellbeing.

New or re-conceived concepts of fun, entertainment and play for people of all ages could be reintroduced within the parks and gardens of the city, providing a 21st century reinterpretation of the pleasure garden. This might include outdoor film screenings, plays and performances, eating and drinking and fireworks in the summer months and illuminations and ice-skating in the winter.

Public spaces within the centre could be utilised for a regular and changing programme of temporary events – including radical and contemporary public art installations by international and local artists, street theatre, dance and musical performances, lighting events, cultural, heritage and community festivals and activities, food festivals, pageants and Mardi Gras, street markets, organised and informal play activities for children and adults, sport, health and wellbeing events, and, in warmer weather conditions, outdoor relaxation and movement classes.

The River Corridor and canal could be animated by art fairs and stalls, boat festivals and racing, cycling events, canoeing and punting and, should water quality allow, river bathing.

A new guide to Bath walks could be promoted to encourage locals and visitors to explore and discover new parts of the city and to venture on foot, by bicycle and public transport to the attractions and countryside beyond the city. The development of Bath as a walkable city could also be directly linked to the NHS Bath and North East Somerset's public health programme, particularly the objective to tackle obesity through active movement and leisure and to the Council's low carbon agenda.

The cultural study produced for the Council by Arts Business Limited, the Destination Management Plan by the Tourism Company, the Retail Strategy by Urban Practitioners, the emerging Bath and North East Somerset Cultural Strategy and the recent Council strategies for sports facilities, green spaces and play should all be integrated into an exciting and radical long-term programme of cultural and community activity, much of which could be played out within the streets and spaces of Bath city centre.

As with the proposals for the physical transformation of the public realm, the opportunity to re-animate and revitalise the centre of the city will need to be a long-term, incremental process. It will require a clear strategy and a planned programme of public and private sector funding and investment. However, properly executed, it has the potential to establish Bath as one of the most attractive and desirable cities in the world.

THE PUBLIC REALM AND MOVEMENT STRATEGY SEEKS TO DELIVER THE FOLLOWING

A more attractive, distinctive, accessible, walkable and user-friendly city centre.

Increased levels of pedestrian and cycling activity across all age ranges covering a wider area of the centre.

Increased levels of economic activity across a wider area of the centre.

A more extensive programme of cultural and community events and activities attracting attendance from local people and visitors and creating a greater sense of social interaction and wellbeing.

Improved access for people with disabilities and mobility impairments.

Improved access and activities for children and young people.

More satisfied residents and local businesses and longer staying visitors and increased visitor spend.

Improved perceptions of Bath.

Enhanced identity and reputation for Bath as a World Heritage Site and world class city.

An enhanced evening and night-time economy.

A safer city centre environment.

London 2012 provides a major milestone for the completion of the first phases of the physical transformation of the public realm and to stage an exciting range of cultural and social events and activities.

However, not all of the opportunities to reanimate the city centre require the physical proposals for a refashioned public realm to be in place. Much could be achieved in the short-term using existing spaces as well as through temporary road closures, enabling local people and visitors to begin to experience the benefits of an active public life and to build towards the cultural programme for 2012 and beyond.

Evening and night-time economy

Well designed streets and public spaces can provide a canvas for public life at all times of the day, including during the evening and at night.

Bath does not benefit from a successful evening and night-time economy and many perceive the city to go to sleep when its shops close at around 5.30pm. Other cities in Europe and beyond have demonstrated that an attractive, accessible and animated centre can attract more people of all ages during the evening and at night, deterring or diluting anti-social behaviour and reducing fear of crime.

While levels of crime and anti-social behaviour within Bath and the rest of the district are relatively low, parts of the city centre suffer from alcohol-related anti-social behaviour at night. This can create a perception of danger which in turn deters some people from visiting after dark.

The Council and its partners are actively seeking to build a stronger evening economy and to reduce anti-social behaviour. A recent success includes the achievement of Purple Flag status for the city centre. This work will continue through council services responsible for the public realm and a range of external partners including Avon and Somerset Police, Future Bath Plus, the business and retail communities and local residents' associations working closely together.

right
Examples of activities, events and animation of public spaces

left
Rynek Glowny Grand Square, Krakow

PART 4:
THE DESIGN ELEMENTS

THE DESIGN ELEMENTS

THE DESIGN ELEMENTS

A Bath Pattern Book will set the future design standards for the city, seeking to capture its DNA as a place and ensuring that all interventions in the public realm embody the city's core design values.

Introduction

The previous sections have presented the key proposals to transform the public realm in Bath and create the broad canvas for public life.

This section focuses on the design elements that will be applied to this canvas, such as hard and soft landscaping, street furniture, lighting, services and facilities, wayfinding products and public art. These elements meet the basic functional needs of the city but they should also reinforce Bath's design values, providing richness, detail and sensory delight to the public realm and strengthening Bath's distinctiveness as a city.

Design philosophy

The emphasis should be about supporting 'Bathness', and will cover functional values (meeting basic needs), inspirational values (does it look like Bath?) and emotional qualities and attributes (does it feel like Bath?). These values will provide a marker to test each intervention, to gauge quality and to ensure that the sense of 'Bathness' is prevalent throughout the design process.

It is also critical that there are tight controls on the number and location of new street furniture, wayfinding and public art products, adhering to the values of 'less is more' and 'lightness of touch'.

Design strategy

The specification of each design element requires a rigorous approach to ensure that they are of the highest quality, and respond appropriately to the city's design values.

This will include an assessment of whole life costs, the consideration of the sustainability impact of design and materials, and ongoing management and maintenance expenditure.

There must be full stakeholder engagement in the selection of design options and materials.

Each design element will be subject to a thorough process of development tailored to suit particular demands.

Audit of existing research available as relevant to each design element.

Commission new research as appropriate to develop knowledge base for design decisions on individual elements.

Analysis of research, and scenario/options testing.

Development of concept design, including user testing and consultation.

Detailed design development, including appraisal of financial implications and sustainability impact.

Consultation, endorsement and inclusion into the Bath Pattern Book.

Training, to ensure proper implementation of the design elements.

Review.

On-going management, maintenance and quality control, necessitating appropriate governance arrangements in the responsible organisations.

Details for other design elements to be included in the Bath Pattern Book will be produced during the first phase of the implementation of the strategy and include the following.

1. Hard landscape elements – paving and street treatment

Original Bath pavements and streets are characteristically paved with pennant, and laid with subtlety and attention to detail; they are understated, recessive and form part of the city's unique composition. We must retain this floorscape character, with paving flags on the pavements and setts in the carriageway, in order to reinforce this special Bath look.

Over recent decades this design tradition has been overlooked with the result that surfacing in many streets and spaces has been undertaken with poor regard to design principles, and using inappropriate materials such as concrete paving slabs and tarmac.

The Bath Pattern Book will propose the use of natural stone to ensure consistency throughout the whole of the city centre. It will be laid in accordance with a limited range of paving patterns. This will apply to both pavements and the carriageway, and will help to reinforce the local distinctiveness of Bath and protect its authenticity as a World Heritage Site.

The Bath Pattern Book will specify the treatment for each street and space within the city centre, and provide specifications for construction, laying and pointing. This will consider opportunities to increase water absorption rates in the context of climate change and increased rainfall.

Although treatment of the streetscape will be tightly controlled, in certain spaces it may be possible to take a more relaxed approach to paving pattern. This will need to be resolved at the detailed design stage.

Existing historic paving and materials are essential characteristics of the city and will generally be retained. There will also be guidance and specifications for the care and maintenance of areas with historic paving, including which mortars should be used and how they should be applied. Training is essential to ensure those undertaking work are suitably skilled.

As the implementation of this strategy will take time to realise, there are likely to be elements within the Plan that will need to be modified as part of routine maintenance work and before natural materials can be afforded. Whilst this will be minimised, with maintenance and budgetary provision coordinated, there will be circumstances where tarmac and concrete paving materials will continue to be used. In the case of existing or new tarmac surfaces in the carriageway, the Bath Pattern Book will seek to ensure that road markings (including yellow lines) are kept to an absolute minimum to reduce visual clutter.

2. Soft landscape elements – trees and woodlands

As well as playing a significant role in defining Bath's landscape setting, trees also make a major contribution to the character of its streets and spaces, to the quality of life of its people and to the biodiversity of the city as whole. Trees connect people to nature and offer shelter and comfort. They provide cleaner air at a time of increasing air pollution as well as shading and cooling.

The arrangement of trees in Bath's public realm is characterised by single mature specimens as in Abbey Green or Kingsmead Square, or groups of trees in spaces such as in The Circus. Trees in key spaces within the city provide important contrast to the architecture of Bath. Views through streets to larger spaces containing trees are generally best left open as they help to reinforce the destination nature of these spaces. The view to Kingsmead Square from its adjoining streets, for example, illustrates this point.

There are opportunities for new tree planting within the proposals. Conversely, tree planting in certain streets and spaces might be inappropriate, where for example tree planting could be said to be working against the architectural purity of the ensemble. The merits, in each case, need to be carefully assessed to ensure that the city's characteristics are enhanced.

It is recommended that a Tree and Woodland Strategy be undertaken for the management of the city's tree and woodland stock. This should consider the issues of the woodlands surrounding the city, as well as identifying actions for existing trees and opportunities for new tree planting. There are also significant opportunities to slow precipitation runoff, provide shading and ameliorate air quality; in order to reduce the impacts which give rise to climate change.

3. Street furniture elements

The city currently hosts a vast range of different products, such as bins, benches, street lights, traffic signs and poles. Each is installed to perform a specific task, but there is very little design consideration over their collective impact.

Whilst some historic street furniture products, including post boxes and the K6 telephone kiosk contribute to the attractiveness of the public realm, the majority of products have been selected on utilitarian grounds with little thought to their contribution to Bath's streetscene. The result is a cluttered environment of poor quality products that detracts from the city's beauty and often interrupts important views. This environment is further eroded by the proliferation of on-street 'A' Boards and there is a need for the Council to produce clear guidance on the future management of these boards within the streetscape.

To achieve a range of products that properly responds to the city's design values, it is recommended that the city should commission its own bespoke suite of street furniture for Bath's city centre. These products will be guided by a series of design values that stem from the 'public realm values and attributes' shown on Page 33. The values dictate that the concept for the products must be:

_fit for purpose
_durable
_finely detailed
_refined
_elegant

This would add another element to reinforce Bath's unique look, avoiding the mixed messages of different street furniture and signage.

A concept design for a wide range of new street furniture products is currently under development. If approved, its delivery can be phased over time, enabled by new development, funding or investment. It is intended that products will include:

_bins, bollards, lighting, seating, cycle racks etc
_a pedestrian wayfinding system
_public transport products including shelters and bus flags

These products will have a clear graphic and information design contained within them, providing a complete city wide system, easily understood by its users and providing the necessary infrastructure for the city to lay claim to its aspiration to become the UK's pre-eminent walkable city. Opportunities to innovate with new products, for example exploring underground waste storage and enhanced recycling facilities, should also be actively explored.

4. Lighting elements

Lighting has many important roles to play in the presentation and enhancement of the city centre. It can play a crucial role in creating a night time environment and economy for the centre, creating an ambience for pedestrians that is safe, comfortable and convivial, as well as exciting and alluring. It can:

_highlight key buildings, streets and spaces and landscape features
_identify walking routes throughout the city helping with the orientation and navigation of the user and linking different parts of the city
_be used to respond to events in the life of the city or particular times of the year. A sophisticated lighting system could be adjusted in intensity in particular areas for specific events or to highlight particular processional routes. At Christmas, a special lighting set could be used to create a magical effect, transforming the city centre and reinventing the concept of Christmas lights

Some key buildings in the city centre and in the surrounding hillsides are already lit, notably the Abbey, Prior Park, Pulteney Bridge and the Holburne Museum of Art.

However there is huge potential to achieve a more sensitive and holistic lighting approach if the city were to commission a comprehensive lighting strategy. This would provide an overall framework and set the tone for the lighting of streets and spaces and specific buildings.

It is suggested that the Lighting Strategy will need to involve leading professional lighting designers and engineers to ensure subtle, high quality solutions which limit light pollution, energy consumption and the impact of light on wildlife (eg. bats). This is yet another opportunity to contribute to the beauty and inherent design quality of the city, and to ensure that the treatment of lighting adds to the unique composition of the place.

Pilot projects could demonstrate the positive effect that an innovative lighting installation can achieve. Bath Street is a good example of an important street that would benefit from such a proposal creating an ambience that contrasts with the main pedestrian retail spine and that connects with the cultural, health and wellbeing epicentre of the Roman Baths and Thermae Bath Spa.

5. Services and facilities

The public life envisaged and promoted by the Public Realm and Movement Strategy will draw more people to enjoy the city centre, increasing footfall and social and economic vitality. This increased activity will be supported by the city's public spaces, parks and riverside as well as the city's shops, cafés, restaurants and cultural offerings. Facilities, such as public conveniences, are also an important part of supporting activity in Bath and making it an appealing destination for visitors.

An increase in public life could highlight the current shortage of accessible public conveniences in the city centre. Bath and North East Somerset Council is currently developing a strategy for public conveniences in consultation with local communities.

The final strategy will deliver a plan to match the demand for publicly accessible toilets in Bath and the district. Its approval will allow early integration with the Local Development Framework and the Public Realm and Movement Strategy.

6. Information and graphic design elements

The development of a graphic and information design language for the city is integral to a new and comprehensive wayfinding system for Bath. It will transform the user experience of the city by seamlessly connecting arrival points (Park and Ride sites, the bus and train stations, and car parks) with pedestrian movement (including websites, maps, interpretation material and directional signage).

The identity for the new graphic and information design language will be guided by the following values:

Information concept
_legible
_intuitive
_reductive/gradual disclosure
_managed complexity
_intelligent

Graphic concept
_formal/mature/confident
_visually rich
_picturesque
_graceful
_engaging
_sensual

The successful integration of a new graphic and information design language for Bath will require the production of detailed brand and identity guidelines, as well as tailored brand management to achieve maximum impact and continuity throughout the city.

7. Public art

The cultural development study carried out for the Council by Arts Business Limited ('Reinventing Bath: a call to leadership and strategic planning to deliver a resort of the future') recommends that the city should produce a Public Art Strategy for Bath as a priority action.

The promotion and implementation of a contemporary arts programme would appeal to new and younger audiences, helping to refresh the image and reputation of Bath as a dynamic and culturally progressive city and to attract new residents, visitors and innovative and creative businesses.

The range of design elements
The DNA of Bath

It is strongly recommended that a Bath Pattern Book for the Public Realm is produced to guide and manage these design elements. This will set the future design standards for the city, seeking to capture its DNA as a place and ensuring that all interventions in the public realm embody the city's core design values. It will extend, refine and refresh the Council's adopted Streetscape Manual as it applies to Bath.

Hard landscaping elements

- Predominately large element pennant paving for footways and small element setts for carriageways laid in accordance with a limited range of paving patterns.
- Very limited use of composite/concrete paving materials.
- Paving typically laid in random width rows using slabs of different lengths.
- Natural stone tactile paving to aid the blind and partially sighted.

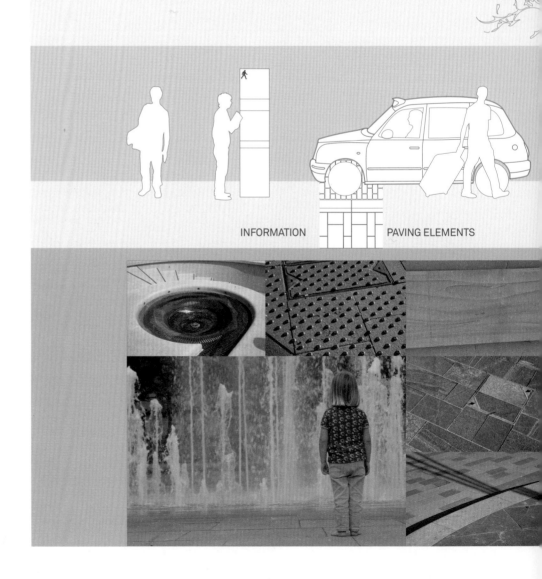

INFORMATION   PAVING ELEMENTS

Soft landscaping elements

– Tree planting.
– Structure/architectural planting.
– Seasonal planting.
– Topiary.

Street furniture elements

– Amenity products – bins, water and drinking fountains, seating.
– Information and wayfinding products – signs, displays, plaques.
– Transportation and highways – bus shelters, bus flags, cycle parking.
– Safety and security – bollards, vehicle control gates.
– Services and utilities – kiosks, utility box covers.

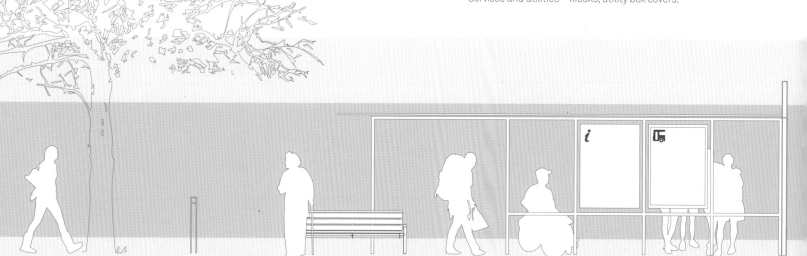

STREET TREES   BOLLARD   BENCH   BUS SHELTER

Lighting elements

- Highways lighting.
- Pedestrian amenity lighting.
- Route lighting.
- Landmark building lighting.
- Feature lighting.
- Product lighting.
- Temporary event lighting.

Public art

- Permanent public art.
- Temporary public art.
- Performance art.
- Interpretation.
- Water and water features used whenever possible as a cross cutting theme.

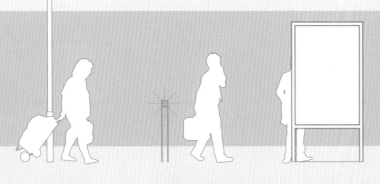

LIGHTING   ROUTE MARKER   EVENTS PROMOTION   PUBLIC ART   DRINKING FOUNTAIN

The Bath Pattern Book for the Public Realm will contain design guidelines, specifications, information planning rules, material specifications, and maintenance and management requirements for the whole range of design elements applied to the public realm.

In addition to the recommended projects, and in response to political will and available resources, other projects that have been outlined in Part 3, Page 45 of the strategy could be implemented at an earlier stage. By necessity any projects selected will need to have acceptable transportation impacts.

This strategy recommends the completion of related strategies, plans and design guidelines that will enable the successful implementation of future projects and inform the treatment of the city's public realm. This phase of preparatory work is essential to ensure that the quality of public realm interventions is appropriate to the quality of the city.

The Bath Public Realm Pattern Book will become a key city management tool, informing and controlling the design quality of proposed projects contained within this strategy.

Graphic elements

- Pictogram set.
- 3D illustration.
- Bath font.
- Photography.
- Colour set.

- Ordnance Survey and royalty free cartography.
- Aerial photography.
- Diagrammatic maps.
- Schematic maps.
- Geographic maps.
- Mental maps.

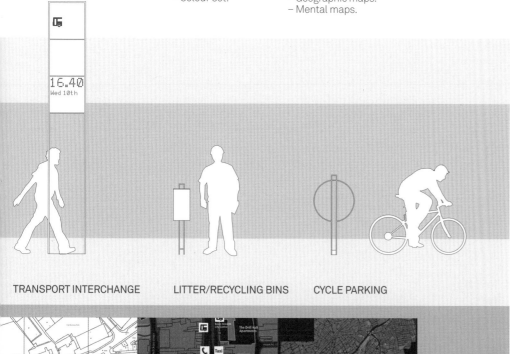

TRANSPORT INTERCHANGE   LITTER/RECYCLING BINS   CYCLE PARKING

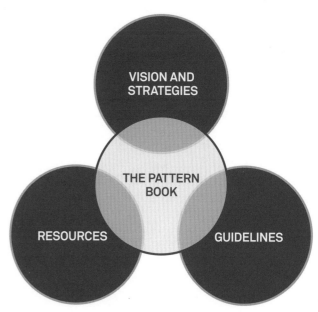

VISION AND STRATEGIES

THE PATTERN BOOK

RESOURCES

GUIDELINES

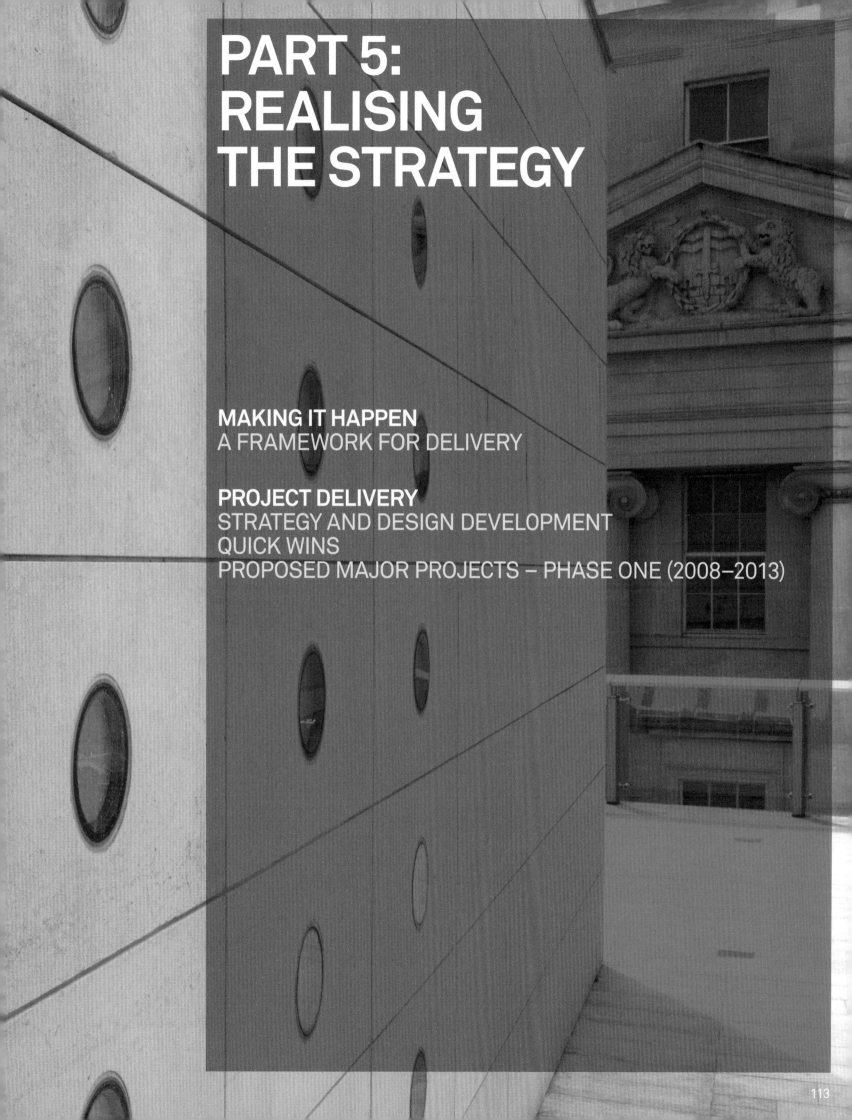

PART 5: REALISING THE STRATEGY

MAKING IT HAPPEN
A FRAMEWORK FOR DELIVERY

PROJECT DELIVERY
STRATEGY AND DESIGN DEVELOPMENT
QUICK WINS
PROPOSED MAJOR PROJECTS – PHASE ONE (2008–2013)

MAKING IT HAPPEN
PUBLIC REALM AND MOVEMENT PROGRAMME

Introduction

This final chapter of the Public Realm and Movement Strategy addresses how the overall strategy is to be delivered.

Public Realm and Movement Programme

A separate document has been produced which outlines a suite of projects that are planned for implementation or are already being implemented under the Council's Public Realm and Movement Programme. The Programme provides a leadership, governance and project management structure for the implementation and delivery of the Public Realm and Movement Strategy. In summary, the Programme currently comprises of the following streams of activity:

Early win projects. These projects seek to tackle issues of immediate concern within the public realm which do not require major capital expenditure and if implemented will demonstrate progress or build momentum towards the delivery of the Preparatory Projects or Transforming Spaces Projects outlined below;

Preparatory projects. These projects seek to design and deliver the public realm products and specifications to enable the Transforming Spaces Projects to be implemented eg. bespoke street furniture, paving, lighting, soft landscaping and a city information and wayfinding system;

Transforming spaces projects. These projects seek to deliver major capital works to incrementally transform the lattice of streets and public spaces across the centre of Bath identified within this strategy.

A five year programme of capital works is provisionally identified in the Council's Capital Programme.

The Public Realm and Movement Programme document is produced as a separate publication to the strategy so that it can be easily updated as further projects are added. These projects will obviously be subject to the identification and approval of appropriate capital and revenue resources, and on the outcome of traffic modelling and other enabling work to facilitate improvements to the transport and movement network.

The success of the first phase of the Public Realm and Movement Programme is also dependent on the initiation of events that complement the physical proposals and which reinforce the use of streets and spaces for public life. These will include cultural and community events including public art, play activities, festivals, live performances and street markets.

A confident city

Intelligent leadership, proper resourcing, and long-term commitment are essential requirements to enable the successful implementation of this strategy, and to build and maintain confidence within the Council and the wider community. Failure to deliver the coherent and integrated components contained in the strategy will undermine the opportunity to achieve the end goal and the competitive advantage and environmental, economic and social benefits that it represents for Bath and the wider area. The realisation of the strategy requires effective cross-service working, cross party political support and long-term buy-in from the wider community if it is to be successfully delivered.

Timescale for delivery

It is proposed that the strategy will be delivered through the phased Public Realm and Movement Programme on an incremental basis over a 10 to 20 year period (or longer if required). Each phase will contribute to the gradual transformation of the city's public realm and be underpinned by a robust movement framework.

The recommended approach to implementation enables the strategy to:

_be achieved as and when resources and opportunities allow
_gives people time to adapt to physical changes, adjust their lifestyles, and experiment with new ways of using the city
_enables greater flexibility in the design process
_allows for continuous review and assessment of progress

The projects within the strategy and programme will be developed in accordance with the Council's comprehensive project management systems and procedures. The programme will seek to ensure coordination with all other relevant council projects and with other projects and activities across the city centre. It will cover a comprehensive range of issues including project development and management, design development, project delivery and ongoing management and maintenance, and will be subject to regular review.

The Programme will be designed to be flexible in order to respond to funding, investment and new development opportunities that may create the conditions for other projects to come forward ahead of schedule. These can be accommodated subject to the necessary transport and movement infrastructure being in place.

It is essential that capital projects are not undertaken without the necessary revenue funding in place to maintain them.

Funding

It is proposed that the strategy will be realised through a range of funding sources including:

_financial contributions arising from new developments
_landowner investment/contributions
_CIVITAS, Bath Package and future transport bids
_Other funding bids such as Growth Points Funding
_potential schemes such as Business Improvement Districts (BIDs)
_access to capital resources as detailed within the Councils property review

The strategy proposes significant levels of investment in high quality projects as appropriate for a World Heritage Site.

As the experience of many cities across the world demonstrates, public sector investment in establishing a high quality public realm significantly enhances a city's ability to attract private sector investment and to generate further economic, cultural and community vitality and success. Money invested by the Council would also benefit the long-term value and sustainability of the commercial estate, which continues to support a range of important Council services.

This strategy can be used as a bidding document and as a contribution to the business case for continuing discussions with the Government and regional agencies. Funding will clearly be required to address significant transportation issues, and the implementation of environmental enhancements to the city's streets and spaces. The strategy also represents a clear statement of intent for continued dialogue with private sector landowners and developers.

Management and organisational structures

Given that the public realm is a complex entity with a vast array of competing demands and interests as well as a plethora of public and private rights, its governance is far from straightforward. The way in which it is managed and promoted will have a huge influence on the appeal and functionality of the city and the ability of this strategy to create the desired conditions for public life.

The proper care and management of the city's physical public realm is of fundamental concern as it can have a profound impact on the user experience of the city. A rigorous and coordinated approach to public realm management is essential. Regular and effective street cleaning, rapid repairs, high-quality maintenance work and the closure of streets for events must all be given high priority to ensure Bath functions successfully.

City management and governance arrangements in Bath need to be tailor-made to ensure that ambitious and cross-cutting proposals are delivered effectively and to a consistently high standard. A sophisticated and comprehensive approach to Design Management is recommended that responds to this challenge, and seeks to ensure that all of the city's design elements add to its unique composition and identity. Bath and North East Somerset Council working in partnership with the private, voluntary, and community sectors has a key role in leading delivery.

The formation of Future Bath Plus, a partnership between the private and public sectors, and the presence of a City Centre Manager has brought increased emphasis on the need to coordinate the delivery of city centre management, tourism and marketing, and cultural provision within the city. Future Bath Plus will have increasing influence over the future running of the city centre and, it is hoped, will support and further develop the ethos and proposals contained within this Public Realm and Movement Strategy.

ACKNOWLEDGEMENTS

The strategy team
The strategy development has been directed and led on behalf of the Cabinet Member and Strategic Director of Development and Major Projects and the Divisional Director of Development and Regeneration by the following team.

Rhodri Samuel
Regeneration Manager/Development and Major Projects/B&NES Council

Stephen George
Senior Urban Designer/
B&NES Council

Mike Rawlinson
Director/City ID

Andy Gibbins
Director/AGA

City ID are the UK's leading design company specialising in city image, identity and legibility. They are Client Lead Design Advisors for the Public Realm and Movement Strategy and associated projects.

The following individuals were led by this team as a core working group for the development of the strategy.

Ruth Burrows
City ID

Nick Durrant
Plot

David Gillam
City ID

Matt Jephcote
City ID

Harriet Miller
City ID

Charles Newall
Property Services/B&NES Council

Jason Smith
City ID

Rab Smith
Transport Policy and Programme Manager/B&NES Council

David Stephenson
Major Projects/B&NES Council

Ben Tappenden
City ID

Michael Thomson
Design Connect

Our thanks also go to the following, who were consulted as specialist advisers on the development of the strategy.

Brian Evans
Gillespies

Andrew Grant
Grant Associates

Les Sparks OBE
URP Member Chairman

The late Honor Chapman CBE
Former URP Member and Vice Chair

Dickon Robinson CBE
URP Member

Prof Chris Baines
URP Member

Alan Baxter
Former URP Member

Sir Richard MacCormac
URP Member

In addition to these individuals we also acknowledge the large number of Bath and North East Somerset councillors and officers who provided valuable guidance and comment at open studio sessions, presentations and on earlier drafts of the strategy. We would also like to thank the following organisations for their input and comments.

Abbey Residents' Association

Avon and Somerset Police

Bath and District Crime Reduction Partnership

Bath and NE Somerset Initiative

Bath and North East Somerset Visitor Attractions Forum

Bath Abbey

Bath Architecture 2008

Bath Bus Company

Bath City Centre Manager Bath Preservation Trust

Bath Chamber of Commerce

Bath Cycling Campaign

Bath Environment Campaign

Bath Federation of Small Businesses

Bath Heritage Watchdog

Bath Royal Literary and Scientific Institution

Bath Society

Bath Tourism Plus

Better Bath Forum

Campaign for Better Transport

Circus Area Residents' Association

Claverton Parish Council

Disability Equalities Forum

English Heritage

Federation of Bath Residents' Associations (FoBRA)

Feilden Clegg Bradley Studios

Future Bath Plus

GWE Business West

Highways Agency

L&R Group

Lansdown Crescent Association

Limpley Stoke Parish Council

London Road Area Residents' Association

National Grid Property (Holdings) Ltd.

Norfolk Crescent Green Residents' Association

Pedestrians Association

Pulteney Estates Residents' Association (PERA)

Royal Crescent Society

Royal United Hospital

Scott Brownrigg

SERA

Somerset County Council

Stubbs Rich

The Coal Authority

The Environment Agency

The Inland Waterways Association

The Theatres Trust

The Woodland Trust

Transition Bath

University of Bath

Wessex Water

WYG Planning & Design

We are particularly grateful to all the individual residents who took the time and trouble to participate in the consultation process.

We apologise if we have accidently omitted any of the organisations which contributed to the consultation process from the above list.

The document
Written and edited by:

Rhodri Samuel
Development and Major Projects/
B&NES Council

Stephen George
Senior Urban Designer/
B&NES Council

Mike Rawlinson
Director/City ID

Andy Gibbins
Director/AGA

Harriet Miller
Lead Designer/City ID

Rab Smith
Transport Policy and Programme
Manager/B&NES Council

Publication designed by City ID.
www.cityid.co.uk

Thank you to the following
organisations and individuals
who have supplied images for
this publication.

B&NES Council: 2, 7–8, 10–11,
26, 101

Bath in Time: 24–29, 94–95,

City ID: 5, 9, 14–16, 26–29, 33,
37–39, 43, 68–69, 73–75, 76–78,
82, 88–93, 100–101, 108–113

Fotohaus: 87

Nick Hand: cover, inside cover,
17, 21, 44–45, 47, 116–117

Colin Hawkins: 8, 34–35

Sophie Laslett: 101

Neill Menneer: 61

Irene Sarda Hervella: 37

Edmund Sumner: 9, 102–103

Thank you to Bath in Time and
B&NES for the images of public life
used to illustrate the timeline.

Thank you to Hess Form & Light for
the images of street furniture used
to illustrate some of the design
elements in this document.

Other photography in this
document has been contributed
by City ID, AGA and Brian Evans.

Cartography, illustrations and
diagrams developed by City ID.

Aerial photography reproduced with
the permission of B&NES Council.

Plans reproduced from Ordnance
Survey with permission of the
Controller of HMSO. Crown
Copyright. B&NES Council licence
number: 10002333

Printed by Park Lane Press on
FSC certified, fully recyclable
On Offset paper, using vegetable
based inks, power from 100%
renewable resources and
waterless printing technology.
Print production systems
registered to ISO 14001: 2004, ISO
9001: 2008 and EMAS standards.

BIBLIOGRAPHY AND REFERENCES

ABL Cultural Consultants (2006) *Reinventing Bath: A Call for Leadership and Strategic Planning to Deliver a Resort of the Future.* Bath and North East Somerset Council.

Alexander, C., Ishikawa, S., Silverstein, M., Jacobson, M., Fiksdahl-King, I., Angel, S. (1978) *A Pattern Language.* USA: Oxford University Press Inc.

Ashworth, G., J. *The Georgian City: the Compact City as Idealised Past or Future Ideal.* Netherlands: Urban and Regional Studies Institute, University of Groningen.

Aymonino, A. and Mosco, V., P. (2006) *Contemporary Public Space: Un-Volumetric Architecture.* Skira.

Bain, M. (2003) *Common Place: Buildings and Spaces that Connect Us.*

Bartlett School of Planning, The, UCL (2004) *Living Places: Caring for Quality.* London: Office of the Deputy Prime Minister.

Bath and North East Somerset Council (2001) *Bath. A City Centre Strategy for Public Art.* Bath and North East Somerset Council.

Bath and North East Somerset Council (2005) *Bath Economic Profile.* Bath and North East Somerset Council.

Bath and North East Somerset Council *Bath Package Major Scheme Bid.* Bath and North East Somerset Council.

Bath and North East Somerset Council (2006) *Bath Package Public Consultation Responses.* Bath and North East Somerset Council.

Bath and North East Somerset Council (2006) *Bath Western Riverside.* Bath and North East Somerset Council.

Bath and North East Somerset Council *BE: Better for Everyone. The Community Strategy for Bath and North East Somerset, 2004 and Beyond.* Bath and North East Somerset Council.

Bath and North East Somerset Council (2006) *City and Town Centres Health Check Study.* Cardiff: Nathaniel Lichfield and Partners.

Bath and North East Somerset Council *Connecting Western Riverside.* Bath and North East Somerset Council.

Bath and North East Somerset Council (2007) *The Future for Bath Vision.* Bath and North East Somerset Council.

Bath and North East Somerset Council *Investing in Bath's Street Furniture Products.* Bath and North East Somerset Council.

Bath and North East Somerset Council (2005) *Living Landmarks Bid.* Bath and North East Somerset Council, Lottery Commission.

Bath and North East Somerset Council (2004) *Local Bus Information Strategy.* Bath and North East Somerset Council.

Bath and North East Somerset Council (2007) *Place Shaping: Public Realm and Movement Strategy.* Bath and North East Somerset Council.

Bath and North East Somerset Council *Public Transport Map 2004–2005.* Bath and North East Somerset Council.

Bath and North East Somerset Council (2006) *Reinventing Bath: A Call for Leadership and Strategic Planning to deliver a Resort of the Future.* Bath and North East Somerset Council.

Bath and North East Somerset Council (2005) *Streetscape Manual.* Bath and North East Somerset Council.

Bath and North East Somerset Council (2007) *Testing Innovative Strategies for Clean Urban Transport: CIVITAS Plus.* Bath and North East Somerset Council.

Bath and North East Somerset Council (2006) *Towards a Place-making Strategy for Bath.* Bath and North East Somerset Council.

Bath and North East Somerset Council (2007) *Transportation, Access and Waste Management: Parking Strategy.* Bath and North East Somerset Council.

Bath and North East Somerset Council (2005) *Walcot Street: Public Realm – Key Issues and Assessment of Potential Projects.* Bath and North East Somerset Council.

Bath and North East Somerset Council, Bristol City Council, North Somerset Council, South Gloucestershire Council (2005) *Provisional Joint Local Transport Plan.*

Bath and North East Somerset Council, Bath City Council, North Somerset Council, South Gloucestershire Council (2006) *Final Joint Local Transport Plan 2006-7 – 2010-11.*

Bath and North East Somerset Council/Planning Services *Archaeology in the City of Bath 2003–2005.* Bath and North East Somerset Council.

Bath and North East Somerset Council/Planning Services (2005) *Bath Citywide Character Appraisal.* Bath and North East Somerset Council.

Bath and North East Somerset Council/Planning Services *City of Bath World Heritage Site Management Plan 2003–2009.* Bath and North East Somerset Council.

Bath and North East Somerset Council/Planning Services (2003) *Western Riverside.* Bath and North East Somerset Council.

Bath City Council (2004) *Caring for Bath.* Bath City Council.

Beaton, M., Chapman, M., Crutchley, A. and Root, J. (2000) *Bath Historical Streetscape Survey Volume 1.* Bath and North East Somerset Council.

Beaton, M., Chapman, M., Crutchley, A. and Root, J. (2000) *Bath Historical Streetscape Survey Volume 2 The Street Histories.* Bath and North East Somerset Council.

de Botton, A. (2006) *The Architecture of Happiness.* Hamish Hamilton Ltd.

Brett, V. (1993) *Pitkin City Guides, Bath.* Norwich: Jarrold Publishing.

Buchanan, P. and Heuman, D. (2004) *Measuring the Benefits of Pedestrian Improvements. Walk 21, Copenhagen Conference Papers.*

Buchanan, C. and Accent, M. R. (2005) *Valuing Walking.*

The Building of Bath Museum (2004) *Obsession John Wood and the Creation of Georgian Bath.* The Building of Bath Museum.

CABE Space (2001) *Living with Risk.*

CABE Space *The Value of Public Space.*

Central London Partnership (2003) *Quality Streets.* Transport for London.

CHORA/Bunscholen, R. (2002) *Public Spaces.*

City-break Guides (2004) *Bath… More than a Guide.* Norwich: Jarold Publishing.

City ID (2006) *Bath Streetscape Options Development.* Bath and North East Somerset Council.

City ID (2006) *Towards a Place-making Strategy for Bath.* Bath and North East Somerset Council.

Commission for Architecture and the Built Environment (2005) *Physical Capital: How Great Places boost public value.*

Commission for Architecture and the Built Environment (2006) *The Value Handbook: Getting the most from your buildings and spaces.*

Commission for Architecture and the Built Environment/DETR (2000) *By Design, Urban Design in the Planning System: Towards Better Practice.* DETR.

Commission for Architecture and the Built Environment/DETR (2001) *The Value of Urban Design.* DETR.

Cowan, R. (2005) *The Dictionary of Urbanism.* Streetwise Press.

Cowan, R. (2002) *Urban Design Guidance.* Thomas Telford.

Dallimore, K. *Exploring Bath.* Millstream Books.

Department of the Environment, Transport and the Regions *Good Practice Guidelines.*

Department of Transport (2007) *Guidance on the Appraisal of Walking and Cycling Schemes.* Department of Transport.

Department of Transport (2007) *Manual for Streets.* Department of Transport.

Dunlop, P. *The Role of Pedestrian Signage in Bath.* Bath and North East Somerset Council, Heritage Services.

Elliott, K. and Menneer, N. (2004) *Bath.* London: Frances Lincoln Limited.

English Heritage (2005) *Streets for All.* English Heritage.

Environment Agency (2002) *Our Urban Future.*

Ernst and Young (2006) *Bath Business Plan.* Bath and North East Somerset Council.

Fawcett, T. (2000) *Paving, Lighting, Cleansing. Street Improvement and Maintenance in Eighteenth-Century Bath.* The Building of Bath Museum.

Forsyth, M. (2003) *Pevsner Architectural Guides: Bath.* Pevsner.

Foster and Partners (1998) *World Squares for All Masterplan.* Foster and Partners.

Gehl, J. and Gemzoe, L. (2000) *New City Spaces.*

Green Spaces (2004) *Street Design.*

Houghton, R. *Reclaiming the Highstreet.*

Jacobs, A. B. (1995) *Great Streets.* The MIT Press.

The Joseph Rowntree Foundation (2007) *The Social Value of Public Spaces.*

Jowell, T. (2005) *Tackling the "Poverty of Aspiration" through rebuilding the Public Realm.*

Keuning Institut and Senza Communicatie (2005) *Shared Space: A Vision for Public Space.*

A Kibblewhite, G. (2004) *The Naked Guide to Bath.* Naked Guides Ltd.

Llewelyn-Davies (2000) *Urban Design Compendium.* English Partnerships and The Housing Corporation.

Lootsma B. and Damen, H. (1996) *A Star is Born: The City as a Stage.*

Lynch, K. (1996) *City Sense and City Design.* The MIT Press.

Lynch, K. (1984) *Good City Forms.* The MIT Press.

Manco, J. (2004) *The Hub of The Circus, A History of the Streetscape of The Circus, Bath.* Bath and North East Somerset Council/ Planning Services.

(2005) *The Bath Magazine.* MC Publishing Ltd.

The Miramar Town Centre Group (2007) *The Miramar Town Centre Pattern Book.*

NEF (2004) *A Wellbeing Manifesto for a Flourishing Society.*

New York City Department of Design and Construction (2005) *High Performance Infrastructure Guidelines.* New York City Department of Design and Construction.

ODPM (2005) *Formulative Evaluation of the Take Up and Implementation of the Wellbeing Power: 2003-2006.* ODPM.

ODPM (2002) *Living Places: Cleaner, Safer, Greener.* ODPM.

O'Rourke, A. (2008) *Place Making. A synthesis of professional practice and case studies about better living environments.* London: RUDI Ltd.

O'Rourke, T., Bath and North East Somerset Council, ICOMOS UK and English Heritage (2005) *Vision for Bath Spatial Framework.* Bath and North East Somerset Council.

Prof. Painter, J. (2005) *Urban Citizenship and the Rights to the City.* Department for Communities and Local Government.

Pattie, C., Seyd, P. and Whiteley, P. (2006) *What is Citizenship? Citizenship in Britain: Values, Participation and Democracy.* Cambridge University Press.

The Planning, Transportation, Economy and Sustainability Overview and Scrutiny Panel (2004) *The Urban Public Realm in Bath and North East Somerset.* Bath and North East Somerset Council.

PEER Workshop, Ghent (2004) *Measuring the Benefit of Public Space Regeneration.*

Snowdon, P. (1997) *Discovering Bath.* Cheltenham: Reardon Publishing.

South West Tourism Research Department (2006) *Bath Visitor Survey.*

Space Syntax (2005) *Bath Western Riverside.*

The Tourism Company (2007) *Bath and North East Somerset Destination Management Plan.* Bath and North East Somerset Council.

Woodward, C. *The Building of Bath.* The Building of Bath Museum.

CONTACTS

Rhodri Samuel
Regeneration Manager
Development and Major Projects
Bath and North East Somerset Council
10 Palace Yard Mews
Bath BA1 2NH

01225 477452
rhodri_samuel@bathnes.gov.uk

Mike Rawlinson
Director
City ID
23 Trenchard Street
Bristol BS1 5AN

0117 917 7000
mike.rawlinson@cityid.co.uk